Guided Paragraph Writing

A first course in English composition
with structural practice

T. C. JUPP and JOHN MILNE

Illustrations by Peter Edwards

HEINEMANN EDUCATIONAL BOOKS
LONDON

Heinemann Educational Books Ltd
LONDON EDINBURGH MELBOURNE AUCKLAND TORONTO
HONG KONG SINGAPORE KUALA LUMPUR NEW DELHI
NAIROBI JOHANNESBURG LUSAKA IBADAN
KINGSTON

ISBN 0 435 28491 6

Published by
Heinemann Educational Books Ltd
48 Charles Street, London W1X 8AH
Filmset by Keyspools Ltd, Golborne, Lancs.
Printed Offset Litho and bound in Great Britain by
Cox & Wyman Ltd, London, Fakenham and Reading

Contents

A much fuller statement of subjects and language learning points will be found at the beginning of each paragraph writing section.

iii

Introduction

The aim of this course is to train students to write a continuous paragraph on straightforward personal topics which will not cause difficulties of content, but will give some opportunity for personal expression. There are eighteen sections each of which is based on a single subject, giving extensive practice with three or four particular structural language points.

Each section is planned as follows:

Oral Practice   Structurally controlled question and answer sequences which involve the student in the section theme and draw out his own experience on the subject, preparing the content of his written work. The teacher will introduce the subject and present the Oral Practice, followed by intensive classroom practice in pairs or groups.

Written Exercises   Further work on the language learning points of the sections. In these exercises there are no unrelated single sentences or constant changes of content. The sentences of each exercise make up a continuous paragraph which is related to the subject of the section.

Sample Paragraph   A sample paragraph on the subject which shows how the work of the Oral Practice and Written Exercises can be put together as a complete paragraph, which also conveys personal information. This is used for further exercises based on rewriting and adaptation of the sample paragraph; practice is thus given with special features of continuous writing such as pronoun reference, tense sequence and sentence connectors.

Vocabulary Study   This provides guidance with vocabulary or usage relevant to the topic. The teacher goes over this, pointing out examples in the section, and then expounding the vocabulary work as appropriate to needs raised by the students. What is provided is intended to stimulate further work on vocabulary.

Student Writing   The student now writes his own paragraph, using the work he has done in these previous sections. He cannot copy the sample paragraph because this is always written in the first person with personal details and local information, which will not apply to the student. The differences between the content of the sample paragraph and what the students will write should be discussed.

Consolidation A variety of further written exercises for immediate follow-up or later revision.

Preliminary Work The language learning points of the sections become more difficult in Parts Two and Three of the course. Some additional preliminary written exercises are provided for classes which require extra practice; but these exercises are not an essential part of the section and can be omitted.

In this course we have tried to present and practise all the language in meaningful situations and give some real opportunity for the student to express himself. As a result the student can develop, even at an elementary stage in his written work, the ability to handle content logically, to master special structural features of continuous writing, and to express his own experiences and ideas. What other reasons are there for learning to write continuous English? Yet most written practice books are still based on unrelated single sentences or closed continuous exercises, in which the student can contribute nothing to the content.

This course is suitable for learners of English with a fairly elementary grasp of the language, or for remedial written work in cases where the student needs a fresh approach to old problems.

In schools where the standard of English is high and composition teaching is given priority, then it should be possible to complete this book in one academic year. But for most average classes, the teacher may find that there is sufficient work in each section for two or even three weeks work. In such situations, it will probably take two years to complete the course.

The course is based on similar principles to the authors' more advanced *Guided Course in English Composition*, which follows on logically from the present book and trains students to write complete compositions. A detailed discussion of the principles and methods underlying both courses will be found in the Teachers Handbook for *Guided Course in English Composition*.

T. C. JUPP
JOHN MILNE

Part One

Only simple sentences are used. Most structural work is on tenses and verb forms. Essential and elementary features of continuous writing such as pronouns and sentence connectors are also dealt with. The subjects for writing about are straightforward and simple.

¶1 Subject: *A Journey*

Write a paragraph about how you travelled to work or school or university yesterday.

LANGUAGE
LEARNING POINTS

Past simple tense
Prepositions of place, time and movement
Pronouns
Verbs of movement

Oral Practice   This practice is to be done orally in pairs or in groups. Every student asks and answers each question.

1   *Question:* What time did you leave home yesterday?
Answer: Yesterday I left home at . . . . (*say the time*)

EXAMPLE: Yesterday I left home at eight o'clock.

2 *Question:* How did you travel?
   Answers: I took a bus to . . . . (*say a place on the way*)
               I went by bicycle to . . . .
               I drove to . . . .
               I walked to . . . .
               I took a train to . . . .

   EXAMPLE: I walked to the bus stop in King's Road.

3 *Question:* What time did you reach . . . .?
      (*say a place on the way and the time you reached there*)

   EXAMPLE: I reached Victoria at eight-thirty.

4 *Question:* Then what did you do?
   Answers: Then I walked to . . . . (*say the place you were going to*)
               Then I caught another bus to . . . .
               Then I took a train to . . . .
               Then I went on foot to . . . .
               Then I pushed my bicycle to . . . .

   EXAMPLE: Then I walked to Parliament Square.

5 *Question:* What time did you arrive?
   Answers: I arrived at . . . . at . . . . (*say place and time*)
               I got to . . . . at . . . .

   EXAMPLES: I arrived at our office at a quarter to nine.
               I got to my school at twenty past nine.

·itten Exercises

EXERCISE ONE Write out the following sentences. Put the verb given in brackets in the past simple tense. You will find the past simple form of these verbs in the Oral Practice.

1 I . . . . home at eight o'clock. (*leave*)
2 I . . . . to the station. (*walk*)
3 I . . . . by train to town. (*go*)
4 Then I . . . . another train. (*take*)
5 I . . . . by bicycle to school. (*go*)
6 Then I . . . . my bicycle into the courtyard. (*push*)
7 I . . . . a bus to X. (*catch*)
   (X is the name of a place you choose.)
8 I . . . . the main street at half-past eight. (*reach*)
9 Then I . . . . another bus to Y. (*take*)
   (Y is the name of another place.)
10 I . . . . a short way and . . . . to my office at a quarter past nine. (*walk, get*)

3

Write out these sentences putting the correct preposition in the blanks. Use either *to* or *at*.

1. I left home . . . . eight o'clock.
2. First I caught a bus going . . . . X.
   (X is the name of a place.)
3. I reached X . . . . eight-thirty.
4. Then I took another bus . . . . Y.
   (Y is the name of another place.)
5. I arrived . . . . Y . . . . nine o'clock.
6. So I got . . . . work . . . . quarter past nine exactly.

Sample Paragraph Read the following passage carefully.

I went to work yesterday as usual. I left home at eight o'clock. First I took a train to Leeds. I reached the Central Station at twenty-past eight. Then I caught a bus to the street corner near our office. I walked a short way and got to work at exactly a quarter to nine.

WORK ON
SAMPLE PARAGRAPH

1. Your teacher may use this passage for dictation.
2. Imagine you made this journey with a friend.
   Write out the Sample Paragraph again beginning the first sentence with X and I . . . . (X is the name of your friend.)
   Then continue with 'we' instead of 'I'.

Vocabulary Study Note the prepositions used in the following expressions:

go *by* car, train, bus, boat	travel *in* a car
go *on* foot	get *on/off* a bus, boat, train
ride *on* a bicycle, donkey, horse	get *out of* a car
travel *on* a bus, train, boat	get *to* school
travel *by* bus, train, boat, car	arrive *at* school

But no preposition is used in these expressions:
enter a compartment (*on a train*)
board a bus, train, boat
drive a car
ride a bicycle, donkey, horse
reach school, work

Student Writing Now write a paragraph like the Sample Paragraph on page 4 to describe your own journey yesterday. If you live in a boarding school or university and do not travel every day, you can describe the journey you made at the beginning of term.

You can use the Oral Practice at the beginning as a guide. Write out an answer to each question so that it is true for you. Then add one or two other sentences and you will find you have written your paragraph.

Correction

1 Read through your paragraph carefully and check it for spelling, correct form of verbs and punctuation.
2 Exchange your work with another student. You check his paragraph for any mistakes and the other student checks your work.
3 Give it to your teacher to read. Remember your teacher would prefer to *read* your piece of writing rather than to *correct* it.

Consolidation This work may be used for revision some time later.

1 Read your own Paragraph One to each other in pairs or in groups.
2 Rewrite the Sample Paragraph again beginning the first sentence with the name of a friend or another student, e.g. Paul went to work . . . .
Then continue with 'he' or 'she' instead of 'I'.

¶ 2

Subject: *The Weekly Holiday*

Write a paragraph about how you spend the morning of yo[ur]
weekly holiday. (Friday, Saturday or Sunday.)

LANGUAGE
LEARNING POINTS

Present simple tense
Adverbs of frequency
Pronouns
Sentence connectors

Preliminary Work   Read these three questions:

Do you have a cup of tea first thing in the morning?
Do you have a cup of coffee first thing in the morning?
Do you have a cup of hot milk first thing in the morning?

Most of the words in these three questions are the same. So the t[hree]
questions can be printed like this:

Do you have a cup of	tea coffee hot milk	first thing in the morning?

You read them in the same way as the three questions printed above. This is called a *substitution table*. In this book some of the exercises will be given in the form of substitution tables.

EXERCISE ONE Write out in full all the sentences in the following substitution table. There are nine sentences.

				brother.
Every	Friday	I have breakfast with my		sister.
	Saturday			
	Sunday			father.

The first one is:

Every Friday I have breakfast with my brother.

Oral Practice This practice is to be done orally in pairs or in groups. Every student should ask and answer each question.

1 *Question:*

What time do you get up at on	Friday?
	Saturday?
	Sunday?

Answer: I get up at . . . . on . . . . (*say time and day*)
EXAMPLE: I get up at nine o'clock on Saturday.

2 *Question:*

Do you have a cup of	tea	first thing in the morning?
	coffee	
	hot milk	

Answers: I have a cup of . . . . first thing in the morning.
I don't have a cup of . . . . first thing in the morning. I have a cup of . . . . (*say what you have*)
EXAMPLE: I don't have a cup of hot milk first thing in the morning. I have a cup of cocoa.

3 *Question:* Do you make your own breakfast or does someone make it for you?
Answers: I make my own breakfast.

My mother	
My sister	
The housekeeper	makes breakfast for me.
My wife	
X	

(X is the person who makes breakfast for you.)

7

4 *Question*: Who do you have breakfast with?
   Answers:

I	sometimes always usually	have breakfast	by myself. with X.

(X is the name of a person.)

EXAMPLE: I sometimes have breakfast with my uncle.

5 *Question*: What do you usually eat for breakfast?
   Answer: I usually eat . . . . for breakfast. (*say what you eat*)

EXAMPLE: I usually eat boiled eggs and toast for breakfast.

6 *Question*: What do you never eat for breakfast?
   Answer: I never eat . . . . for breakfast. (*say what you never eat*)

EXAMPLE: I never eat chocolate biscuits for breakfast.

7 *Question*: What do you do after breakfast?
   Choose an answer or make up one of your own:

   I have a bath.
   I clean the house.
   I listen to the radio.
   I read the newspapers.

8 *Question*: Do you go out during the morning?
   Answer:

I	sometimes occasionally always	go out to	meet . . . . visit . . . . walk . . . . play . . . .

EXAMPLE: I sometimes go out to play football with my friends.

9 *Question*:

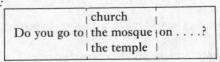

Do you go to	church the mosque the temple	on . . . .?

Answer:

I	sometimes always occasionally	go to	the mosque the temple church	on . . . .

EXAMPLE: I sometimes go to church on Sunday morning.

Written Exercises

EXERCISE TWO   Write out one sentence from each of the following substitution tables. Complete the sentence by putting the verb given in brackets in the present simple tense. X is any name you choose.

1

X usually . . . . at about	eight o'clock		Friday.	
	half-past eight	every	Saturday.	(get up)
	nine o'clock		Sunday.	

EXAMPLE: Mary usually gets up at nine o'clock every Sunday.

2   Then he/she always . . . . a bath. (have)

3

Her sister/mother	
His friend	usually . . . . the breakfast. (make)
The boarding-house cook	

4

They . . . . some	cheese	and then they . . . . some	tea.	(eat,
	eggs		coffee.	drink)
	fish		hot milk.	
	toast		(etc.)	
	(etc.)			

5

After that X	a newspaper.
	a book.
	(etc.)

(read)

6   Or sometimes he/she . . . . the radio. (listen to)

7

Later on	he	often . . . . out	to see some friends.	
	she		to visit his/her aunt.	(go)
			to play football.	

8

Or sometimes	he	. . . .	to church.
	she		to the mosque.
			to the temple.

(go)

EXERCISE THREE   The following paragraph was written by answering each question in Exercise Two. Read this paragraph and complete the answers to the questions after it.

Mary usually gets up at about nine o'clock on Sunday. Then she always

9

has a bath. Her mother usually makes the breakfast. They eat some toast and drink some coffee for breakfast. After that Mary reads a newspaper, Or sometimes she listens to the radio. Later on she often goes out to walk in the park with friends. Or Sometimes she goes to church.

1 Does Mary *sometimes* get up at about nine o'clock?
   Answer: No, she *usually* gets up at . . . .
2 Does she sometimes have a bath?
   No, she always . . . .
3 Does her mother always make the breakfast?
   No, she . . . .
4 Does Mary always listen to the radio?
   No, she . . . .
5 Does Mary ever go out to walk in the park?
   Yes, ...
6 Does Mary never go to church?
   No, ...

Sample Paragraph   Read the following passage carefully.

Every Sunday morning I get up at half-past nine. My wife makes the breakfast straight away. We have breakfast together. We usually have a boiled egg each and some toast and we drink some coffee. After that we sometimes clean the house and always read the newspaper. Later on we often go out and visit a friend or relation.

WORK ON SAMPLE PARAGRAPH
1 Your teacher may use this passage for dictation.
2 Write out the Sample Paragraph again beginning:
   'Every Sunday morning X gets up at half-past nine.'
Use any name you choose and make all the necessary changes to 'I', 'my' 'we' and to the verb forms.

Vocabulary Study   *Meals*
At what time of day do you usually have breakfast, lunch, tea and dinner in your country?
Here is a breakfast menu from a London hotel. Do you know the meaning of the different items on the menu?

What would a breakfast menu be like in a hotel in your country? Write one out.

Grand Hotel

21st November, 1972

<u>Breakfast</u>

Fruit Juice
or
Cereal

Kippers
or
Bacon & Eggs
(or Eggs boiled, poached, fried, etc.)

Tea or Coffee

Sunday activities

Here is a list of some of the things people do in England on a Sunday morning. Study this list and make a list of your own of the things people do on the weekly holiday in your country.

go to church	do the housework
read newspapers	wash the car
sleep very late	take the dog for a walk
work in the garden	go out walking
write letters	go to the pub at lunch-time

Student Writing Now write a paragraph of ycur own to describe how you spend the morning of your weekly holiday. Use the Sample Paragraph, the Oral Practice and the Written Exercises as a guide to help you write your paragraph. Use these words to connect your sentences

Then . . . ., After that . . . ., Later on . . . .

Correction

1 Read through your paragraph carefully and check it for spelling, correct form of verbs and punctuation.

2 Exchange your work with another student. You check his paragraph for any mistakes and the other student checks your work.

3 Give it to your teacher to read.

Consolidation This work may be used for revision some time later.

1 Read your corrected Paragraph Two to each other in pairs or in groups.

2 Go back to the Sample Paragraph on page 10 and write it out again.
This time change the first sentence to:
   Last Sunday morning I got up at half-past nine.
and continue with all the verbs in the past simple tense.
Leave out the words:
   'sometimes' 'always' 'often' and 'or relation'

3 Exchange your own corrected paragraph with another student and read or write out the other student's paragraph putting in his or her name instead of 'I' and make all the necessary changes to the verb forms and the pronoun forms.

FURTHER WORK Mr. Hardy is a very lazy and greedy man. Using the Sample Paragraph and Written Exercise Two as a guide, write out the story of how Mr. Hardy spends his holiday morning.
Remember Mr. Hardy gets up very late.
         He eats a lot for breakfast.
         Someone else cleans his house.
         He goes back to bed after breakfast.
Use 'then' 'straight away' 'after that' 'later on' to relate your sentences.
Add one or two sentences of your own.

¶3 Subject: *Yesterday Evening*
Write a paragraph about how you spent yesterday evening.

LANGUAGE
LEARNING POINTS

LANGUAGE
LEARNING POINTS

Past simple tense
Pronouns
Negatives
Sentence connectors

Oral Practice

This practice is to be done orally in pairs or in groups. Every student should ask and answer each question.

1 What time did you arrive home yesterday evening?

I arrived home at . . . . (*say the time*)

2 What did you do then?

I

had a wash.
had a rest.
read the newspaper.
made some tea.

3

Do you live
- alone?
- with your family?
- in a boarding house?

I live . . . .

4 Who makes your evening meal for you?

I make my evening meal myself.
My mother/sister/wife (etc.) makes my evening meal.

5 What did you do after that?

After that
- I went out.
- I went with my friends.
- I read a book.
- I read the newspaper.
- I did my homework.
- I talked to . . . .

6 What did you do later?

Later
- I went to the cinema.
- I watched television.
- I read a book.
- I did my homework.
- I visited . . . .
- I talked to . . . .

7 What time did you get back home?

I didn't go out.
I got home at . . . . (*say the time*)

8 What time did you get to bed?

I got to bed at about . . . . (*say the time*)

Written Exercises

EXERCISE ONE   Write out one sentence for each of the following substitution tables and put the verb given in brackets in the past simple tense. X is any name you choose.

1

Yesterday evening X . . . . home at	half-past four. five o'clock. half-past five. six o'clock.	(*get*)

14

2

				to read a book.
Straight away he . . . . a cup of	tea	and . . . . down	to watch television.
(have)	coffee	*(sit)*	to do his homework.

3

	. . . . the book		six o'clock.	*(read)*
He	. . . . television	until	half-past six.	*(watch)*
	. . . . his homework		seven o'clock.	*(do)*

4

Then he . . . . a wash and a meal and	. . . . out with his friends.	*(go)*
(have)	. . . . television.	*(watch)*

5 They . . . . to the café/to the cinema. *(go)*
He . . . . television all evening. *(watch)*

6

Later		. . . . to bed early.	*(go)*
After the film	X	. . . . home at ten o'clock.	*(get)*

7 Finally he . . . . asleep at about eleven o'clock. *(fell)*

EXERCISE TWO   Answer the following questions in a way that is true for you.
EXAMPLE: Yesterday evening did you get home at half-past five?
     Yes, I did.
     No, I did not. I got home at quarter-to-seven.

1 Yesterday evening did you get home at six o'clock?
Yes, I did.
No, I did not. I got home at . . . .

2 Did you have a cup of tea?
Yes, I did.
No, I did not. I . . . .

3 Did you watch television?
Yes, I did.
No, I did not. I . . . .

4 Did you read a book?
Yes, I did.
No, I did not. I . . . .

5 Did you have a bath?
Yes, I did.
No, I did not. I . . . .

15

6 Did you go out?
Yes, I did.
No, I did not. I . . . .

7 Did you do your homework?
Yes . . . .
No . . . .

8 Did you play cards with your friends?
Yes . . . .
No . . . .

9 Did you go to the cinema?
Yes . . . .
No . . . .

10 Did you get to bed at half-past nine?
Yes . . . .
No . . . .

Sample Paragraphs Read the following passages carefully:

A Yesterday evening I got home from work at six o'clock. My mother made my tea and I ate it straight away. After that I sat down and watched television for about an hour. Then I went to my room and read some chapters of an interesting book. Later some friends called. We chatted for some time and my mother brought us all some cocoa. My friends left at ten o'clock and, after a bath, I went to bed.

B This paragraph was written by answering each question in Exercise One beginning on page 14.

Yesterday evening Peter got home at half-past four. Straight away he had a cup of coffee. Then he did his homework until seven o'clock. At seven o'clock he had a wash and a meal, and after that he went out with his friends. They went to the cinema. After the film Peter got home at ten o'clock. Finally he went to bed at about eleven o'clock.

WORK ON SAMPLE PARAGRAPHS

1 Your teacher may use Sample Paragraph A or Sample Paragraph B for dictation.
2 Rewrite Sample Paragraph A beginning:
'Yesterday evening Mary got home from work at six o'clock'.
Use any girl's name you choose.
Make the necessary changes to 'I' 'my' 'me' 'we' and 'us'.

3   Rewrite Sample Paragraph B. Change each sentence into the negative and then add a sentence as in the example below. Change the name 'Peter' to another name.

EXAMPLE:

Yesterday evening George did not get home at half-past four. He got home at seven o'clock.

Make any other changes to the times given.
Leave out the words 'straight away' 'then' 'after that' 'after the film' and 'finally'.

Get

The word 'get' is used in English with many meanings. It is used here with the meaning of 'arrive' or 'move'. It often suggests completion of the movement.

get home	get out of (the room etc.)
get back	get in (the car etc.)
get to work	get into (the car etc.)
get to bed	

(Some further examples are given in Vocabulary Study in Section One on page 4.)

'get' also means 'become'.
For example: get cold, get dark, get bigger, etc.

'get' can also mean 'receive'.
'He gets £17 a week,' means, 'He receives £17 a week as his wages.'

Evening activities

Here is a list of some of the things people do in England in the evening. Study this list and make a list of your own of the things people do in the evening in your country.

at home:	watch television	do the housework
	read books	invite friends for a meal
	prepare for work the next day	invite friends for coffee
go out:	to the cinema	to a pop concert
	to the theatre	to visit friends
	to a concert	to the pub

Student Writing   Now write a paragraph of your own saying what you did yesterday evening. Use the Sample Paragraphs, the Oral Practice and the Written Exercises as a guide to help you write your paragraph. Use these words to connect your sentences:

'then' 'after that' 'later' and 'finally'.

Correction

1 Read through your paragraph carefully and check it for spelling, correct form of verbs and correct form of pronouns.

2 Exchange your work with another student. You check his paragraph for any mistakes and the other student checks your work.

3 Give it to your teacher to read.

Consolidation This work may be used for revision some time later.

1 Read your corrected Paragraph Three to each other in pairs or in groups.

2 Read your own corrected Paragraph Three again and underline all the forms of the personal pronoun that you have used: 'I' 'me' 'my' etc.

3 Complete the following table with a form of the pronoun similar to those given in the first line:

I   *me*   *my*
you
he
she
we
they

4 Use words like 'after that' 'straight away' 'finally' 'later' and 'then' to complete the blanks in the following paragraph. Before you begin, study how these words are used in the Sample Paragraphs on page 16.

Sandra got home at five o'clock. . . . . she had a bath and . . . . she made a meal. . . . . she washed up and cleaned the sitting room. . . . she watched television for an hour. . . . she put out the lights and went to bed.

¶ 4

Subject: *Yourself*
Write a paragraph describing yourself. Say what you look like, what you do and where you live.

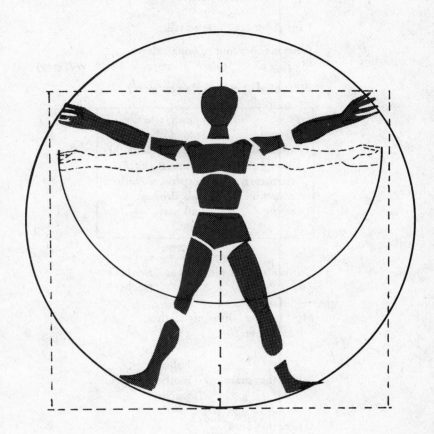

LANGUAGE
LEARNING POINTS

Present simple tense
Verb + present participle
Prepositions
Negatives

Oral Practice   This practice is to be done in pairs or in groups. Each student should ask and answer each question.

1   How old are you?
I am . . . . years old.

19

2　What height are you approximately?

I am
- very tall.
- quite tall.
- not very tall.
- of medium height.

or

I am about .... metres tall.

3　What is the colour of your hair?
My hair is .... (*black, brown, fair, blonde, red, grey*)

4　What kind of clothes do you wear?

I	always usually often frequently sometimes never	wear	new clothes. old clothes. fashionable clothes. unusual clothes. expensive clothes. silk dresses. silk saris. (etc.)

5
Do your clothes please your
- father?
- mother?
- teacher?

My
- father
- mother
- teacher
likes my clothes.

or

My clothes make my
- father
- mother
- teacher
angry.

6　Where do you
- study?
- work?

I am a student in .... (*say where you study*)
I work in .... (*say where you work*)

7　What do you like doing in your spare time?

I	like dislike enjoy	going to the cinema. playing football/netball/etc. chatting with my friends. listening to pop records. sitting in the cafe. going to political meetings. (etc.)

8 Where do you live?
I live in . . . . (*say the town or district*)

9   alone?
Do you live   with your family?
                 with friends?

I live . . . .
I share a flat with . . . .

ten Exercises

XERCISE ONE   Write out the following passage putting the correct preposition in the blanks. Choose from:
    with, in, to, on, of

Sandra is 17 years old and about 1·7 metres tall . . . . long, black hair. She works . . . . a shop all day and usually goes out . . . . her friends . . . . the evening. She likes listening . . . . pop records . . . . the café. She lives . . . . three friends . . . . a large flat. She has lots . . . . interesting pictures . . . . the walls . . . . her bedroom.

XERCISE TWO   Write out the following sentences putting the verb in brackets in the present simple tense. Complete these sentences in either the affirmative or negative, *whichever is true for you.*

EXAMPLE: I . . . . expensive clothes. (*wear*)
            I wear expensive clothes.
    or I do not wear expensive clothes.

(a)   I . . . . brightly coloured dresses. (*wear*)
(b)   I . . . . in my spare time. (*work*)
(c)   I . . . . a lot of pocket money every week. (*get*)
(d)   I . . . . going to political meetings. (*like*)
(e)   I . . . . sitting in the café by myself. (*enjoy*)
(f)   I . . . . with my family. (*live*)
(g)   I . . . . in the college hostel. (*live*)

Complete this form in pairs. One student pretends he is an official asks another student his name etc. and writes down the answers. Then second student acts as the official and does the same.

STUDENT'S RECORD CARD
COMPLETE IN BLOCK CAPITALS

FAMILY NAME	COLOUR OF HAIR (brown, black, red, fair, etc.)
OTHER NAMES	COLOUR OF EYES (blue, green, black, etc)
ADDRESS	SCHOOL OR COLLEGE
SEX	SUBJECTS STUDIED
AGE LAST BIRTHDAY	SPORTS
HEIGHT	HOBBIES

Sample Paragraph   Read the following passage. It was written by a young university stud in England.

I am eighteen years old, not very tall and I have long black hair. I w very unusual clothes and my father often gets angry with me. He wa me to wear a suit and a tie. I am a student at Leeds University and I w hard before the exams. In my spare time I like sitting in the studer union and chatting with my friends. During term I share a flat with th friends. I have a lot of bright posters on the walls of my bedroom.

22

1   Your teacher may use this passage, or part of it, for dictation.
2   This passage was written by a student called Bill. Rewrite this passage beginning:
     'Bill is eighteen years old . . . .' Make all the necessary changes in the verb forms and to the pronoun forms: 'I' 'my' 'me'.

bulary Study   Make sure you know the different names for the clothes worn by men and women.

A man wears a shirt	A woman wears a blouse
a tie	a jumper
a pullover	a dress
a suit	a skirt
trousers	a mini-skirt
jeans	a tunic
(etc.)	a maxi-skirt
	trousers
	jeans
	a trouser suit
	nylons
	tights
	(etc.)

Boys and girls both wear school uniform.
Who else wears a uniform?
Men and women both wear shoes, sandals, boots.
What other articles of clothing are the same for men and women?
What are the students in your class wearing?
Find out the correct spelling in English of any local or national dress which is worn in your country.

dent Writing   Now write a paragraph like the Sample Paragraph to describe yourself: what you look like, what you do and where you live. Use the Oral Practice, the Written Exercises and Sample Paragraph as a guide to help you write your paragraph.

Correction
1   Read through your paragraph carefully and check it for spelling, correct form of verbs and correct form of pronouns.
2   Exchange your work with another student. You check his paragraph for any mistakes and the other student checks your work.
3   Give it to your teacher to read.

Consolidation This work may be done sometime later as revision.

1 Read your corrected Paragraph Four to each other in pairs or in grou

2 Study the following sentence from the Sample Paragraph.

In my spare time I *like sitting* in the students' union and *chatting* my friends.

Look through your own paragraph to see if you have used verbs like 'en 'hate' 'like'.

EXERCISE FOUR Write out the following sentences with the verb in brackets in the cor form. Make the sentence positive or negative so that *it is true for you*.

1 I like (go) to the cinema.
2 I dislike (watch) football matches.
3 I hate (do) nothing.
4 I enjoy (sit) by the fire in winter.
5 I like (wait) for a bus in the rain.
6 I dislike (eat) ice-cream.
7 I like (wear) old clothes.
8 I enjoy (visit) friends.
9 I hate (write) letters.
10 I dislike (wash) the car in winter.

FURTHER WORK Here is some information about Miss Milne. Using the Sample Paragr and Exercise One as a guide write a short paragraph describing her.

Miss Milne is eighteen years old
1·7 metres tall
she has short, curly hair
sometimes wears very colourful dresses
is a student at college
enjoys reading magazines in her spare time
hates doing nothing
often spends her money on her friends
lives with her family in . . . . (*any place you choose*)
has her own room with lots of interesting photogra from magazines on the walls

24

¶ 5 Subject: *The Next Public Holiday*

Write a paragraph describing how you will spend the next public holiday.

**LANGUAGE
ARNING POINTS**

Future tense
Prepositions
Joining sentences with same subject
Pronouns
Revision of present simple and past simple tenses

Oral Practice This practice is to be done in pairs or groups. Each student should ask and answer each question.

1 What is the next public holiday?

	Christmas.
	New Year.
The next public holiday is	Diwali.
	Id El Ramadan.
	Mardi Gras.

(or the name of the next holiday in your country.)

25

2   When will it be?
     It will be on . . . . (*say the date*)

3   Will you go to work on that day?
     No, I shall not go to work.
     Yes, I shall go to work.

4   Will you give anyone presents on that day?

Yes, I shall give my
- father
- mother
- brother
- sister
- aunt
- friends (etc.)

a present.

No, it is not the custom to give presents on that day.

5   What will you give
- him?
- her?
- them?

I shall give my
- aunt
- sister
- friend (etc.)

. . . . (*say what you will give*)

I shall not give anyone a present.

6   Will anyone give you a present?

Yes, my
- father
- mother
- friend (etc.)

will give me a present.

7   Will you buy new clothes for the holiday?

Yes, I shall buy a new
- dress.
- shirt.
- pair of trousers. (*or say what you will buy*)
- pair of shoes.
- hat.

8   Will you do anything special before breakfast?

Yes, we shall
- go to church
- go to the mosque
- go to the temple (etc.)

before breakfast.

9   What will you do after breakfast?

After breakfast
- I shall go and visit my friends/relatives.
- my friends/relatives will come and visit me.
- I shall . . . .

26

10   What will you do later?

	go for a picnic.
	prepare a special lunch.
	go to the zoo.
Later we shall	walk in the park.
	go in a boat on the river.
	listen to the bands playing.
	go to the fair.

11   Will you have any special food on that day?
Yes, we shall have . . . .
(*say the name of a special food you will have*)

MATICAL NOTE   In this lesson we have used 'shall' after 'I' and 'we', and 'will' in all other cases. You should practise this. But in modern English 'will' is often used instead of 'shall'.

ritten Exercises

EXERCISE ONE   Write out the following passage putting the verbs given in brackets in the future tense with 'shall' or 'will'.

The next public holiday (be) the Late Summer Bank Holiday. It (be) on Monday the 30th August. On that day I (get up) early and I (not go) to work. I (put) on some old clothes and we (have) breakfast early. Then I (go) to the bus station with the rest of my family. We (catch) a bus to Southsea and we (go) to the seaside. At Southsea we (play) on the beach and swim in the sea. Later we (have) a huge meal of fish and chips.

EXERCISE TWO   Write out the following passage putting the correct preposition in the blanks. Choose from the following:
   with, on, at, in, to, for

The next public holiday will be the Id El Kibir. I shall get up early . . . . the morning and go . . . . the graveyard . . . . my mother. We shall take some fruit and some sweets . . . . us and leave them . . . . the graves. Later we shall go back . . . . our house and drink coffee . . . . the rest of our family. My father and brother will kill a sheep and prepare it . . . . cooking. After breakfast my father and brother will go . . . . the mosque and my mother and I will stay . . . . home and prepare the special lunch.

XERCISE THREE   Join the following pairs of sentences in the way shown in the examples.

EXAMPLES:
I shall get up early. I shall put on my clothes as quickly as possible.
I shall get up early and put on my clothes as quickly as possible.

I shall call on a friend. We shall go to the park.
I shall call on a friend and we shall go to the park.

27

Where the subject of both sentences is the same, you do not repeat th
subject and you leave out 'will' or 'shall'.

Where the subject of both sentences is different, you must write out bot
subjects in full with 'will' or 'shall'.

1 On Mardi Gras I shall get up early.
   I shall put on my best clothes.
2 My friends will be waiting at the street corner.
   We shall go to the Main Square.
3 We shall stand in the Main Square.
   We shall wait for the band.
4 The band will come by.
   Lots of people will follow it.
5 We shall join the people behind the band.
   We shall march with them through the town.
6 The older people will watch from their windows.
   We shall march in the street.
7 The mayor will make a speech in front of the town hall.
   There will be lots of singing and dancing.
8 Later we shall have a rest.
   We shall eat a huge meal of pumpkin pie.
9 In the evening we shall watch the fireworks.
   We shall dance until early morning.
10 We shall go home very late.
   We shall sleep all the next day.

Sample Paragraphs Read the following passages carefully.

A This paragraph was written by a schoolboy in England.

The next public holiday will be Easter Monday. This year it will be o
the 12th of April. I shall get up early and meet my friend, Ronnie. W
shall get a train into the centre of the city. Then we shall go to the Enginee
ing Exhibition in the Queen's Hall. After that we shall go to the fair o
Woodhouse Moor. We shall spend all our money at the fair. We shall e
all sorts of things—things such as chips, hot dogs, and candy floss. We sha
probably meet friends there. I shall go on the dodgems and have a try
the shooting stall. In the evening we shall catch the last train and get hom
very late.

DIFFICULT WORDS *engineering exhibition*: a show of engines and machinery.
fair: shows and entertainments which come to a place at a public holida
chips: fried potatoes
hot dogs: hot sausages in bread rolls
candy floss: a kind of sweet

28

dodgems: electric cars; you try to bump into other cars
shooting stall: a place where you shoot air guns to win prizes.

B   This paragraph was written by a schoolgirl in the Sudan.

The next public holiday will be the Id El Ramadan. We shall finish fasting on the last day of Ramadan and be ready to eat as much as possible on the first day of the Feast. All our family will have new clothes and we shall get up early to put them on. I shall go with my mother and visit my grandmother in her house. Later we shall come back home and have a special breakfast. After breakfast I shall go out with my cousins to the park. We shall sit there and drink pepsi cola and listen to the transistor radio. Later I shall go home for lunch. We shall have lots to eat on that day.

WORK ON
ᴍᴘLE PARAGRAPHS

1   Your teacher may use part of the Sample Paragraphs for dictation.
2   Paragraph A was written by a boy called Stan. Rewrite this paragraph from the third sentence beginning:
    Stan will get up early and meet his friend, Ronnie.
    Make all the necessary changes to the pronoun forms 'I' 'my' 'we' 'our' and to 'shall'.
    Note: 'we' becomes 'they' and 'our' becomes 'their'.
3   Paragraph B was written by a girl called Leila.
    Rewrite this paragraph from the fourth sentence beginning:
    Leila will go with her mother and visit . . . .
    Make all the necessary changes to the pronoun forms 'I' 'we' and 'my' and to 'shall'.

Vocabulary Study   Here is a list of some of the things people often do in England on special holidays. Make a list of the things people do in your country.

Christmas:
Give and receive presents
Have a Christmas tree with presents tied to it
Open presents in the morning
Children play with toys
Go to church
Eat a special meal of turkey and Christmas pudding
Go to a pantomime (a special play for children)
Play in the snow
Sing songs

29

Easter Sunday:
Roll coloured eggs in the park
Eat coloured eggs for breakfast
Girls wear new clothes, especially new hats
Walk in the park

Easter Monday and Summer Bank Holiday:
Go to the seaside
Go on a picnic
Go to an exhibition
Go to the fair
Go to the cinema
Eat ice cream and fish and chips

Student Writing Now write a paragraph describing what you will do on your next public holiday. Use the Oral Practice, the Written Exercises and the Sample Paragraphs as a guide to help you write your paragraph.

Correction
1 Read through your paragraph carefully and check it for spelling and correct use of 'will' and 'shall'.
2 Exchange your work with another student. You check his paragraph for any mistakes and the other student checks your work.
3 Give it to your teacher to read.

Consolidation This work may be done sometime later as revision.
1 Read your corrected Paragraph Five to each other in pairs or in groups.
2 Go back to Sample Paragraph A on page 28 and rewrite it from the third sentence beginning:
Every Easter Monday Stan goes and meets his friend, Ronnie. They . . . .
Change all the verbs to the present simple tense.
Make sure you use the correct form.
Make all the necessary changes to the pronoun forms 'we' and 'our'.
3 Go back to Sample Paragraph B on page 29 and rewrite it from the fourth sentence beginning:
'Last Id El Ramadan Leila went with her mother . . . . ,
Change all the verbs to the past simple tense.
Make sure you use the correct form.
Make all the necessary changes to the pronoun forms 'I' 'we' 'my'.
Look back to Sample Paragraph One on page 28 for guidance.

¶6 Planning

Planning of Subject Matter

1 Read through the Sample Paragraph in Section One on page 4. The subject matter is in the order that things happened:

I left home *at eight o'clock*.
First I took a train.
I reached the town centre *at twenty-past eight*.
Then I caught a bus . . . .

When you are writing *a narrative*, arrange your subject matter in the order of the times at which the different things happened.

2 Now read through the Sample Paragraph in Section Four on page 22. Is the subject matter in this paragraph arranged in the same way as the subject matter in the Sample Paragraph in Section One?

You can see that it is not. This is because the Sample Paragraph in Section Four is *a description* and not a narrative. In a description there is no order of time. For a description the best way to arrange your subject matter is to put together all the sentences about the same thing:

age, height, colour of hair, the clothes you wear: *description of yourself*.
studies and spare-time activities: *what you do*.
live in Copenhagen East, your room: *where you live*.

Written Exercises

EXERCISE ONE Mrs. Williams is a school teacher. Here is a list of some of the things she does during the day. The items in the list are not in order. Arrange these items in order.

What she does	The time
has lunch	12.45
starts teaching again	2.00
has a cup of tea during break	11.00
leaves the house	9.00
has breakfast	8.30
stops teaching	12.15
arrives at school	9.20
starts teaching	9.30

EXERCISE TWO Mr. Wood is very lazy. Here are some sentences that can be used to describe him. The items in the list are not in order. Arrange these items in order.

has pictures of food on the walls of his room
has red hair

31

gets up late
lives in York
goes to bed in the afternoon
has green eyes
is 1 metre tall
eats four or five times a day
sleeps between meals
watches television
has very short hair
lives in a large house with three servants

Student Writing *Either* write a paragraph on what Mrs. Williams does during her working day.
Use the list in Exercise One to help you. Do not use *all* the times given but use 'First' 'Then' etc. Refer back to the Sample Paragraph in Section Two on page 10 for further guidance.

Or write a brief description of Mr. Wood. Use the list in Exercise Two on page 31 to help you.
Join some of the items with 'and'. Refer back to the Exercises and Sample Paragraph in Section Four on pages 19 to 22 for further guidance.

Correction
1 Read your paragraph carefully and make sure the subject is well arranged.
2 Exchange your work with another student who has written about the other subject. That is, if you have written about Mr. Wood, exchange your paragraph with a student who has written about Mrs. Williams. Check what the other student has written.
3 Give your paragraph to your teacher to read.

Part Two

Complex sentences containing
adverbial clauses of time and
adjectival clauses are introduced.
There is also a variety of work on
verb forms, articles, prepositions
and pronouns. The subjects are
more difficult, but still mainly
narrative. Letter writing is
introduced.

Supplementary written structural
practice is given in the form of
preliminary work before each
section. These exercises are not an
essential part of the preparation for
writing and can be omitted with
students who have no special
difficulty with the structures dealt
with.

Simple grammatical notes are
provided for students who are
interested, but again these are not
an essential part of the text.

¶ 7

Subject: *An Unhappy First Visit*

Write a paragraph about your first day at school, or your firs
visit to hospital, or your first visit to any place or person which
you disliked very much.

LANGUAGE Time clauses
LEARNING POINTS Past simple tense
Past continuous tense
Passive voice

Preliminary Work

EXERCISE ONE Join the following pairs of sentences as in the examples.

EXAMPLES: I first went to the cinema. (*when*) I was five years old.
I first went to the cinema when I was five years old.

(*when*) The lights went out. I felt afraid.
When the lights went out, I felt afraid.

1 I first went to the dentist. (*when*) I was seven years old.
2 (*when*) I entered the waiting-room. I felt afraid.
3 I went into the dentist's surgery. (*when*) The receptionist told me.
4 (*when*) I sat in the large chair. I shut my eyes.

34

5　(*when*) I opened my eyes.　The dentist was laughing.
6　He held me firmly.　(*when*) I cried out with pain.

　These sentences can be divided into two parts.
The part which begins with 'when' is called a *time clause*.
The other part is called the *main clause*.
Notice the use of the comma (,) when the time clause comes first.

Oral Practice　Decide what you will write about before you begin these exercises.

Ask and answer the following questions and make up sentences from the substitution tables.

1

How old were you when you first went to	X's house? school? work? college? a cinema? the dentist? the doctor? a police station? hospital? Y (*the name of a town*)? a funeral?

I was . . . . years old when I first went to . . . .
　　(*say your age*)　　　　　　　　(*say where you went*)
EXAMPLE: I was ten years old when I first went to a funeral.

2　Did you go to . . . . alone or with someone?

I went to . . . . by myself.

I went to	with	my grandfather. my mother. my brother. some friends. 　　(etc.)

EXAMPLE: I went to the funeral with my mother.

3

Did you feel	afraid unhappy frightened terrified horrified shy nervous	when you went to . . . .?

When I went to . . . ., I felt . . . .

EXAMPLE: When I went to the cinema, I felt afraid.

35

4

I was most frightened by
the darkness.
the huge building.
all the policemen.
the strange faces.
the medical instruments.
the crowds in the street.
(etc.)

5

When
the lights went out,
I sat in the dentist's chair,   I felt very . . . .
I entered the playground,
(etc.)

EXAMPLE: When I entered the playground, I felt very nervous.

6   What happened next?

Then I
looked for my friend's house.
was given an anaesthetic.
was given an injection.
shut my eyes.
ran out of the playground.

7   What happened after that? (*choose one answer*)
I watched the rest of the film in silence.
I began to enjoy the film.
I ran out of the playground.
The dentist started to drill my teeth.
I got lost.
(*or whatever happened*)

8   What happened in the end?
I came out of the cinema quite happy.
I ran home.
I asked a stranger the way.
(*say what happened to you*)

Written Exercises

EXERCISE TWO   Write out the following sentences and put the verb given in brackets
the past simple tense.

School
1   I first (go) to school when I (be) five years old.
2   When I (enter) the playground, I (feel) very afraid.
3   I (look) for another way out.
4   I (run) home as fast as possible.

The dentist

5 Peter first (visit) the dentist when he (be) eight years old.
6 He (become) afraid when he (see) the man in the white coat.
7 When the dentist (tell) him to sit down, he (begin) to shake.
8 When the dentist (finish) his inspection, Peter (jump) out of the chair immediately.

EXERCISE THREE   Rewrite the following sentences in the passive voice.
EXAMPLES: The strange smell frightened me.
                I was frightened by the strange smell.

                They took him into the hospital.
                He was taken into the hospital.

When you rewrite the sentences, leave out any word in italics.

Hospital

1 A car knocked John down.
2 *They* took him to hospital in an ambulance.
3 *They* put him onto a wheeled stretcher.
4 *They* pushed him down a long corridor.
5 The strangeness of the place frightened John.
6 *They* took him to the X-ray room.
7 Later a nurse took him to a ward.
8 *They* put him into bed.
9 His parents visited him some hours later.
10 *They* allowed him to go home after a few days.

Paragraphs   Read through the following passages.

A   I first went to school when I was five years old. I did not want to go, but my grandfather held my hand firmly and I was taken to the school gate. When I went into the playground by myself, I was frightened by all the strange faces and the large, ugly building. I quickly found another gate on the other side of the playground. I got out by this gate and ran home. When my grandfather arrived home a little later, he was surprised to find me. I was sitting by the fire quite happy.

B   My first visit to the cinema was a very unhappy one. I was taken there by some friends when I was only seven years old. At first there were bright lights and music and I felt quite happy. When the lights went out, I felt afraid. Then the film started and I saw a train on the screen. The train was coming towards me. I shouted out in fear and got down under my seat. When my friends saw me, they started to laugh. I felt ashamed and sat back in my seat. I watched the film to the end but I still felt afraid. I was glad when the film ended.

1   Your teacher may use part of the Sample Paragraphs for dictation.
2   Rewrite Sample Paragraph A beginning:
> William first went to school . . . .

Use any name of a boy and make all the necessary changes to the pron▸
forms.
3   Rewrite Sample Paragraph B beginning:
> Susan's first visit to the cinema was . . . .

Use any name of a girl and make all the necessary changes to the pron▸
forms.
4   Notice the use of the past continuous tense.
In Sample Paragraph A:
> I *was sitting* by the fire quite happy.

In Sample Paragraph B:
> The train *was coming* towards me,

Now rewrite the following passage putting the verbs given in bracke▸
the past continuous tense.

When I (walk) down the street, I heard a shout. A small boy (shout)
help. He (hold) his stomach. A car (pass) and I stopped it. When we (d▸
to the hospital, the boy (cry) with pain. When we got to the hospital, s
nurses (wait). They (take) him away when I remembered to ask his n
and address. I went to his parents' house and they immediately wer
the hospital. Two weeks later I met the boy again when I (walk) to w
He thanked me for my help.

Vocabulary Study

A   Here is a list of words which tell you how you feel when you don't
something:

unhappy	terrified
afraid	troubled
frightened	puzzled
horrified	

You can use some of these when you write your paragraph.

B   Find out the words you need to use to tell about your first unhappy ▸
For example:

a doctor
a dentist   has   a receptionist
a waiting-room
a surgery

in a hospital there are the wards, an operating theatre, an X-ray roo▸
in a cinema there is the screen, the audience.
at a funeral there are the mourners, the body, the coffin.

38

Now write a paragraph of your own to describe your first unhappy visit. Use the Oral Practice, the Written Exercises and the Sample Paragraphs as a guide to help you write your paragraph.

Correction

1 Read through your paragraph carefully and check:
   (a) correct use of the passive voice;
   (b) correct use of past continuous tense.
2 Exchange your work with another student. You check his paragraph for any mistakes and the other student checks your work.
3 Give it to your teacher.

Read your corrected Paragraph Seven to each other in pairs or in groups.

Rewrite the following passage putting the verbs given in brackets in the correct form. Use either the past simple or past continuous tense. Use the passive voice where it is required.

My first time at a funeral

When I (be) ten years old, my uncle (die). It (be) my first time at a funeral. My mother (buy) me a new suit and I (walk) to my uncle's house. He (lie) in a coffin. I (feel) very afraid and upset. The priest (say) a long prayer and the coffin (close). My aunt and some other women (weep). The coffin (lift) up and (take) out to a waiting car. When we (arrive) at the cemetery, the coffin (take) out of the car and (carry) to the grave. When it (lower) into the ground, the priest (say) some more prayers. After that we all (go) home. I (be) very glad when the funeral (finish).

Here is the answer to Exercise Four. Notice where the past continuous tense and the passive voice are used.

Answer to Exercise Four

When I was ten years old, my uncle died. It was my first time at a funeral. My mother bought me a new suit and I walked to my uncle's house. He was lying in a coffin and I felt very afraid and upset. The priest said a long prayer and the coffin was closed. My aunt and some other women were weeping. The coffin was lifted up and taken to a waiting car. When we arrived at the cemetery, the coffin was taken out of the car and carried to the grave. When it was lowered into the ground, the priest said some more prayers. After that we all went home. I was very glad when the funeral finished.

¶ 8

Subject: *Unexpected Money*

Imagine that you have received a sum of money unexpected either by inheriting it or winning it in a competition or lotte or by getting it in any other way. Write a paragraph saying h this happened and what you did with the money.

Time clauses and tenses
Past perfect tense
Articles
Prepositions
Pronouns

Vocabulary Study   Before you begin work on this section make sure you know the mean of the following:

imagine : think of something not true.

But do *not* imagine your story if you can write about a true one.

to inherit money : to receive money from a relative or a friend who has died.

a will : a piece of writing in which a person says what he wants done with his property and money after he dies.

a raffle, a lottery : you try to win money by buying a ticket which you hope will be picked as the winning ticket. A raffle is usually smaller than a lottery.

to gamble : to play a game for money or win money on the result of a sport.

:liminary Work

MATICAL NOTE
EXERCISE ONE

In Section Seven you practised time clauses beginning with 'when'. Time clauses can also begin with 'after' 'before' and 'while'.

Rewrite the following sentences and where a verb is given in brackets:

(a) rewrite it in the past simple tense in a time clause beginning with 'when';

(b) rewrite it in the past continuous tense in a time clause beginning with 'while';

(c) rewrite it in the past perfect tense in a time clause beginning with 'after';

(d) rewrite it in the past perfect tense in the main clause where the time clause begins with 'before'.

Winning a competition

1 After I (complete) the competition, I put the entry form in an envelope.
2 Before I put it in the envelope, I (read) my answers again and again.
3 After I (post) the letter, I waited for two weeks.
4 I felt very hopeful, while I (wait).
5 After I (wait) two weeks, I received a reply.
6 While I (open) the envelope, my hands were shaking.
7 When I (open) the letter, I found a prize of £20.
8 My father (go) out before I received the letter.
9 I told him the good news when he (come) home in the evening.
10 After I (tell) him, he took the money.

MATICAL NOTE

The past perfect tense in sentences with 'after' and 'before' emphasises strongly that one thing happened after or before the other. If there is no need for this emphasis then the past simple tense can be used in both parts of the sentence.

For example, Sentence 2 in the above exercise can be:

Before I put it in the envelope, I *read* my answers again and again.
and Sentence 7:

After I *read* the letter, I felt very excited.

41

Oral Practice

1   Use the following substitution table to make up sentences:

Recently		inherited	
Three months ago	I unexpectedly	won	.... *(say the amount*
Last week		got	*of money)*
Last year		found	
		made	

2   Ask each other the following questions and answer them from the substitu-tion tables:

	inherit	
	win	
How did you	get	this money?
	find	
	make	

	an aunt.
	an uncle.
I inherited this money from	a friend of the family.
	(etc.)

or	I won the money in	a raffle.
		a lottery.
		a competition.
		a football pool.

			working in the holidays.
	made		selling vegetables.
or	I got	the money by	selling an old record-player.
	earned		betting on ....
	won		(etc.)

3   Had you wanted anything for a long time?

	inherited		a radio.
	won		a television.
Before I	earned	this money, I had always wanted	a car.
	got		a bicycle.
	made		a sewing machine
			(etc.)

42

4 How did you feel?

When I	got the letter, heard the news,	I felt very	excited. happy. anxious. glad.

5 How did you spend some of the money?

I spent some of the money on	clothes. books. school fees. a party. (etc.)

6 How did you spend the rest of the money?

I bought presents for my	brother sister mother friends	with the rest of the money.

Written Exercises

EXERCISE TWO   Join the following pairs of sentences using 'when' 'after' 'before' and 'while' and put in pronouns as shown in the examples.

EXAMPLES: (After) Tom had worked for two weeks.
Tom received £25.
After Tom had worked for two weeks, he received £25.

(when) Tom told his parents.
Tom's parents were very pleased.
When Tom told his parents, they were very pleased.

1 (while) Tom was waiting to go to university.   Tom found a job.
2 (when) Tom told his mother.   Tom's mother was very pleased.
3 (after) Tom had worked for two weeks.   Tom got £25.
4 (when) His friends heard this.   His friends were very pleased.
5 Tom had put £15 in the bank.   (before) Tom told his friends.
6 (when) His father heard this.   His father congratulated him.
7 (after) Tom had arranged a party.   Tom invited his friends.
8 (when) Mary heard about this.   Mary wanted to come.
9 Tom had invited Mary.   (before) Mary asked him.
10 (after) Tom's friends had enjoyed themselves at the party.
Tom's friends thanked him warmly.

43

EXERCISE THREE   Study the following passage carefully, then rewrite it putting the verbs in brackets in the correct tense and in the passive where necessary. Note that the past continuous tense and the past perfect tense can be used in sentences without 'while' 'before' or 'after'.

While Hassan (shop) in the market one day, he (hear) a man shouting. The man (sell) lottery tickets. Hassan (buy) one before he (go) home. When the result of the lottery (announce) a few days later, Hassan (be) extremely happy. He (win) a small prize of £15. When he (receive) the money, Hassan (go) straight to a radio shop. He (buy) a transistor. While he (walk) home, he (turn) on the radio and (listen) to his favourite programme.

Sample Paragraphs   Read through the following passages:
A   Three months ago I unexpectedly inherited £100. I inherited this money from a cousin of my mother's after she had died. She had left me the money in her will. When I heard the news, I was waiting to go to university and I did not have enough money for new clothes and books. After I had received the money, I went out shopping. I bought a new suit and some shirts and a new pair of shoes with part of the money. Also I bought some books. I bought a cigarette lighter for my father and a bottle of perfume for my mother. After I had bought everything, I had £20 left. When I came back, I showed them the clothes and the books and gave them the presents.

B   Last year I saw a competition in a newspaper. There were photographs of twenty beautiful girls. You had to choose the three most beautiful girls and write a sentence about each one. I decided to enter the competition. After I had waited for three months, I was very surprised to receive a letter. I had won a prize of £25. At that time I was saving up to buy a motor cycle. When I got this £25, I had enough money for the motor cycle. I took all the money and bought my new motor cycle. I had passed my driving test before I started saving. I was able to drive away immediately. While I was driving through the town on my new motor cycle, I felt very happy and excited.

WORK ON   Study the following sentences taken from the Sample Paragraphs and note
SAMPLE PARAGRAPHS   the words in italics.

Sample Paragraph A
I bought *a* new suit and *some* shirts and *a* new pair of shoes.
I bought *a* cigarette lighter for my father and *a* bottle of perfume for my mother.
When I came back, I showed them *the* clothes and *the* books and gave them *the* presents.

Sample Paragraph B
At that time I was saving up to buy *a* motor cycle.
When I got this £25, I had enough money for *the* motor cycle.

44

Note When writing a paragraph we use 'a' or 'some' when we first mention someone or something. Later when we write about the same person or thing we use 'the' or we can use 'this' or a pronoun.

EXERCISE FOUR   Write out the following passage completing the blanks with 'a', 'an' or 'the' 'the'.

Last week I entered . . . . competition. . . . competition was quite easy. You had to study . . . . picture and in . . . . picture there were some mistakes. You had to write these mistakes in . . . . list and send . . . . list to . . . . newspaper. . . . newspaper announced the results after five weeks. I had won . . . . prize. When I received . . . . prize, I was very happy. It was . . . . fountain pen. I showed . . . . fountain pen to my brother and he was quite jealous.

EXERCISE FIVE   Write out the following sentences and put the correct prepositions in the blanks.

1   I inherited this money . . . . a cousin . . . . my mother's.
2   She had left me the money . . . . her will.
3   I did not have enough money . . . . new clothes and books.
4   I bought a new suit and some shirts and a new pair . . . . shoes . . . . part of the money.
5   I bought a cigarette lighter . . . . my father and a bottle . . . . perfume . . . . my mother.
6   Last year I saw a competition . . . . a newspaper.
7   You had to write a sentence . . . . each photograph.
8   I had won a prize . . . . £25.
9   . . . . this £25 I had enough money to buy the motor cycle.
10   While I was driving . . . . the town . . . . my new motor cycle, I felt very happy and excited.

Note: The answers to 1–5 can be found in Sample Paragraph A and to 6–10 in Sample Paragraph B.

Vocabulary Study   Study the Vocabulary Note at the beginning of this Section on page 40, and ask your teacher about any words you need to write your paragraph.

Student Writing   Now write a paragraph of your own telling how you unexpectedly received some money.
Use the Oral Practice, the Written Exercises and the Sample Paragraphs to help you write your paragraph.
Try to use some sentences containing time clauses.

45

Correction

1 Read through your paragraph carefully checking the tenses and forms of the verbs you have used and also the punctuation in sentences containing time clauses.
2 Exchange your work with another student. You check his paragraph for any mistakes and the other student checks your work.
3 Give it to your teacher to read.

Consolidation

1 Read your corrected Paragraph Eight to one another in pairs or in groups. Discuss any mistakes you have made.
2 *A Competition*
Use the following to arrange a competition in your class.

The artist drew Picture One and after he had drawn it he drew it again and made some changes. The changes are shown in Picture Two. Study the pictures and find out the changes.

How to enter the competition:
Write your name at the top of a sheet of paper.
Write six sentences about the changes.

EXAMPLE: After he had drawn a man, he changed it to a woman.

This is the first change. Now write another six sentences all in the same way:

After he had drawn a . . . ., he changed it to a . . . .

When each student has written six sentences on his piece of paper, fold the papers and collect them together.

Put the papers in a box and mix them together. One student picks out a paper and opens it up. If there are six correct sentences on the paper, this paper is the winner and gets first prize of £15. If there is any mistake the paper is put aside and another paper chosen.

The second correct paper gets a second prize of £10 and the third paper a third prize of £5.

When the three prize winners have been chosen, then each winner must tell the class what he would like to do with this imaginary money.

(*For correct answers see page 72.*)

Subject: *An Unwelcome Meeting*
Preliminary work about Adjectival Clauses.

EXERCISE ONE Join the following pairs of sentences in the way shown in the examples.

EXAMPLES: A few weeks ago someone came to visit us.
He was an old friend of my father.
A few weeks ago someone *who was an old friend of my father* came to visit us.

One day I met a man in the street.
He wanted to borrow some money from me.
One day I met a man in the street *who wanted to borrow some money from me.*

GRAMMATICAL NOTE If the adjectival clause relates to the subject of the first sentence (as in Example One) it comes immediately after the word it relates to:
A few weeks ago someone *who was* . . . .
If the adjectival clause relates to the object of the first sentence it comes at the end of the first sentence:
. . . . a man in the street *who wanted* . . . .

1 Last night I sat beside a man in a café.
He talked all the time about his family.
2 Last night a man sat beside me in the café.
He talked all the time about his health.
3 A few weeks ago someone came to our door.
He was a friend of my brother.
4 One evening a young man came to the door.
He wanted to sell me a new dictionary.
5 A few nights ago I sat beside a woman in the cinema.
She talked all the time during the film.
6 One morning I sat beside a man on the bus.
He complained all the time about the bus-service.
7 Last month I met a woman on the train.
She talked all the time about her garden.

GRAMMATICAL NOTE In these sentences the adjectival clause tells you who the person is. They are *defining* adjectival clauses. They are *not* separated by commas from the rest of the sentence.

Join the following pairs of sentences in the way shown in the examples:

> EXAMPLES: Peter called at our house. He talks all the time.
> Peter, who talks all the time, called at our house.
>
> I went to visit my grandfather last night.
> He always talks about his early life.
> Last night I went to visit my grandfather, who always talks about his early life.

1 My grandfather came to visit me. He likes to give advice to everyone.
2 Last week I met Mr. Smith. He is a well-known bore.
3 Tom came to visit me last night. He usually wants to play his records.
4 A few nights ago in a café I met Peter. He always tries to borrow money.
5 My father's boss came to visit us. He always talks about very uninteresting subjects.

GRAMMATICAL NOTE In these sentences you know who the person is and the adjectival clause just gives you some extra information. They are *non-defining* adjectival clauses and are separated by commas from the rest of the sentence.

¶ 9

Subject: *An Unwelcome Meeting*
Write a paragraph about an occasion when you met someone
who was boring or frightening or a nuisance.
(*a nuisance:* someone who causes you trouble.)

LANGUAGE
LEARNING POINTS

Adjectival clauses defining and non–defining with 'who' as subject.
Revision of tenses in time clauses
Tenses in adjectival clauses
Verbs used to emphasise repetition
Catenatives: He *refused to* go.

Oral Practice

1   Use the following substitution table to make up sentences.

One	morning afternoon evening	about	two three four (etc.)	days ago weeks ago months ago	I was sitting alone	at home. in a café. in a bus. in a train. in the park. (etc.)

EXAMPLE: One evening about three weeks ago I was sitting alone in a café.

50

2 Ask each other the following questions and answer them from the substitution tables.

What were you doing?

	listening to the radio.
	watching television.
	reading a book.
I was	studying for an examination.
	writing letters.
	doing my homework.
	sleeping.
	(etc.)

3 If the person was not known to you:

Who	came to the house?
	spoke to you?

A man	who wanted to talk about	his	health	came to the door.
A woman		her	family	sat down beside me.
			business	

or

Someone who	wanted to sell me	came up to me.
	asked me a lot of silly questions	

If the person was known to you:

Mr. X,	who is a well-known bore,	came to the door.
My uncle,	who likes giving people advice,	sat down beside me.
X,	who talks all the time,	came up to me.
	who always wants to borrow money,	
	books,	
	records,	

4 What did you do?

I tried to be polite.
I listened patiently for half an hour.
I smiled.
I pretended to be deaf.
I asked him/her to come in/go away.

51

5 What did the other person do?

He	went on talking.
She	kept on talking.
Mr X	refused to stop talking.
My mother's friend	did not go away.
(etc.)	

6 What happened in the end?

I asked him/her to leave the house.
I pretended to be sick.
I got up and left the cinema/train/bus.
I moved to another seat.
My parents came home.

Written Exercises

EXERCISE THREE   Read the following passage carefully and then rewrite it joining the pairs of sentences printed in italics with a 'who' clause as in Exercises One and Two on pages 48 and 49.

One evening I was sitting in a café drinking a cup of coffee. *A man came in and sat down beside me. He looked very odd.* He began talking about his health. He went on and on and he was very boring. *A friend came into the café. He was meeting me.* I got up quickly, excused myself and joined my friend.

EXERCISE FOUR   Rewrite the following passage putting the verbs in brackets in the correct tense.

One evening a few weeks ago while I (sit) alone at home reading a book, someone (knock) at the door. When I (open) it, I found a stranger. The man who (stand) at the door (want) to sell me some brushes. I (not have) any money and also we (not need) any brushes. I (ask) him politely to go away. The man, who (look) rather poor, (keep) on talking. Finally I (be) rude. I (order) him to go away. When he still (go) on talking, I (close) the door in his face. After I (wait) some moments, I (hear) him pick up his case of brushes and go away. I (go) back to my chair and (begin) reading again.

GRAMMATICAL NOTE   Note the use of the following verbs followed by *to* + infinitive.

The man *wanted to sell* me some brushes.
I got into an empty compartment and *started to read*.
I *pretended to have* a friend in the restaurant car.

Other verbs followed by *to* + infinitive in the same way are:

begin	have	love	promise	
continue	hope	mean	refuse	wish
decide	learn	offer	remember	
forget	like	prefer	try	

52

Rewrite the following sentences in the way shown in the example.

> EXAMPLE: He talked about his health. (*start*)
>   He started to talk about his health.

1 He talked about his family. (*begin*)
2 He had five children. (*pretend*)
3 He had two more (*hope*)
4 He showed me photographs of his childeren. (*promise*)
5 I listened to him for another minute. (*refuse*)
6 I stopped the conversation. (*try*)
7 I read my book in silence. (*wish*)

le Paragraphs Read through the following passages.

A Last summer I went to visit an aunt who lives in Scotland. I went by train. The train was not very full and I got into an empty compartment and started to read. Just before the train left the station, a young man, who looked like a businessman, got into the same compartment. Shortly after the train started, he began to talk. He talked about his work and went on telling me about the people who bought cars from him in many different towns and cities. I became very bored. I pretended to have a friend who was in the restaurant car. I took my book and went to the restaurant car and stayed there for the rest of the journey.

B A friend, who lives some distance from me, came round one evening with his cousin. My friend went to a meeting and left his cousin with me. This man, who had never met me before, began talking about a book. The book was very uninteresting, but he went on talking about it. I tried to change the subject of the conversation, but he kept on talking about this dreadful book. When I offered him some coffee, he refused but I insisted and escaped into the kitchen. I was very glad when my friend, who luckily was not kept long at the meeting, returned. They both had some coffee and left quite early. I was very pleased when they left.

WORK ON
PARAGRAPHS
1 Write out the sentences in Sample Paragraph A and in Sample Paragraph B which contain adjectival clauses beginning with 'who'. There are four sentences in Sample Paragraph A and three sentences in Sample Paragraph B. Underline the adjectival clauses.

53

Vocabulary Study

A   Note the use of the preposition 'about' in the following expressions:
  to talk *about* someone or something:
    He talked about his health.
    He talked about his friends.

  to tell someone *about* someone or something:
    He told his father about his problem.
    He told me about his brother.

B   There are different ways of emphasising that someone continued to something for a long time.
  (*a*) repetition of the verb:
    He talked and talked and talked.
    He studied and studied and studied.
  (*b*) use of 'keep on' + present participle:
    He kept on talking.
    He kept on running.
  (*c*) use of 'go on' + present participle:
    He went on writing.
    He went on asking me questions.
  (*d*) use of 'on and on' referring back to an earlier verb:
    I stopped walking but he went on and on.
    No one liked his singing but he went on and on.

C   Can you see the difference between?

  'a boring man' and 'a bored man'
  'an interesting man' and 'an interested man'

  If you rewrite these with adjectival clauses you get:

  a boring man: a man who bores other people
  an interesting man: a man who interests other people

  Here the verb in the adjectival clause is in the active voice.

  a bored man: a man who is bored by something or someone
  an interested man: a man who is interested by something or someone

  Here the verb in the adjectival clause is in the passive voice.

EXERCISE SIX   Rewrite the following expressions with adjectival clauses in the way show above.

  a frightening man—a frightened man
  a pleasing child—a pleased child
  a surprising man—a surprised man
  a terrifying man—a terrified man
  an exciting person—an excited person

54

Now write a paragraph of your own telling how you met someone who was boring or troublesome. Use the Oral Practice, the Written Exercises and the Sample Paragraphs to help you write your paragraph.

Try to use some sentences containing adjectival clauses beginning with 'who'.

Correction

1 Read through your paragraph carefully checking your punctuation and your use of adjectival clauses.

2 Exchange your work with another student. You check his work for any mistakes and the other student checks your work.

3 Give it to your teacher to read.

Consolidation

1 Read your corrected Paragraph Nine to one another in pairs or in groups. Discuss any mistakes you have made.

2 Write out the following passage:

(a) putting the verbs in brackets in the correct tense;

(b) punctuating the passage in a suitable way.

One morning last week i (get) on the bus on my way to work i (sit) beside a woman who (carry) a large shopping basket she (start) to talk about her shopping she (go) on and on i (see) someone who (use) to work in the same office as me he was sitting further up the bus i (excuse) myself and (go) and (join) him the woman who (be) such a bore (begin) talking to the next person who (sit) beside her

55

PRELIMINARY
¶ 10

Subject: *An Interesting Place to Visit*
Preliminary work about adjectival clauses.

EXERCISE ONE   Complete the sentences with *who* or *which*. *Who* is used to refer to peop[
and *which* to things.

Heathrow Airport, London

1   Heathrow Airport, ... is one of the busiest airports in the world, is
the west side of London.
2   The aeroplanes . . . . land there come from most countries in the world.
3   The people . . . . sit in the large terrace café can watch the aeroplar
landing and taking off.
4   The announcements . . . . are made over the loudspeakers are in ma
different languages.
5   The passengers . . . . arrive from abroad must go through customs.
6   In the airport there are many shops . . . . sell all kinds of things . . . . a
useful for travellers.

EXERCISE TWO   In defining adjectival clauses *that* can be used instead of *who* or *whi*
Substitute *that* for *who* or *which* where possible in Exercise One.

GRAMMATICAL NOTE   In Section Nine and in Exercises One and Two of this paragraph you ha
practised adjectival clauses like this.
There are many shops *which* sell all kinds of things.
In these sentences the relative pronoun (*who*, *which*, *that*) is the subject
the adjectival clause.

In this sentence the relative pronoun is the object of the adjectival claus
The people who you see at the airport come from all over the world.

The relative pronoun can be left out of a defining adjectival clause of tl
type.
The people you see at the airport come from all over the world.

In non-defining adjectival clauses the relative pronoun cannot be left o
Whom (or *who*) is used for a person and *which* for a thing.
Mr. Smith, whom you met yesterday, is a friend of my father's.
Stratford-on-Avon, which many tourists visit every year, is well-knov
for the Shakespeare Memorial Theatre.

If necessary, complete these sentences with: *who, whom, which, that.* Where the relative pronoun can be left out, write out the sentence without any change.

The Science Museum, Kensington, London

1 The Science Museum, ... I have often visited, is a most interesting place.
2 The museum contains machines and inventions .... great scientists made in the past.
3 Some of the engines .... you can see there were made many years ago.
4 One of the most interesting things .... you can see is the first steam engine.
5 Models of engines .... may be made in the future are also on show.
6 There are also models of engines .... you can start by pressing a button.
7 Scientific theories .... I have never understood before are clearly shown in coloured diagrams and models.
8 There are many interesting books .... you can buy in the bookshop .... contain photographs of trains and boats and engines.

¶10

Subject: *An Interesting Place to Visit*

Write a description of a place you know which is worth visiting. Choose any place you like, such as a city, a museum, a historical building, a river, an airport or a factory.

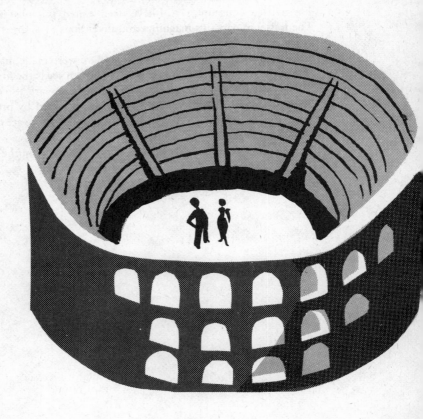

LANGUAGE
LEARNING POINTS

Adjectival clauses:

defining and non-defining with 'which' as subject

defining and non-defining with relative pronoun as object (usually omitted in defining clauses)

Oral Practice   Ask and answer the following questions:

1 What sort of place do you like to visit?

The sort of place I like to visit is	a museum.
	an airport.
	a place by the sea.
	a beautiful city.
	an historical ruin.
	an exhibition.
	(etc.)

2 Where are you going to write about?

The place I am going to write about is . . . .

EXAMPLE: The place I am going to write about is an ancient Greek city called Cyrene.

3 Where is Y? (Y is the name of the place in Question 2.)

It is in . . . .
It is about . . . . kilometres from . . . .

EXAMPLES: The Kensington Science Museum is in West London.
Cyrene is about 300 kilometres from Benghazi.

4 How can you get there?

There is a	poor good modern	bus service train service road	to	and Y is near	the railway station. the bus stop. an underground station. the crossroads.

5 What happens when you get there?

When you get there,	you can stay in a hotel.
	you will be met by a guide.
	you must buy an admission ticket.
	you can have lunch in the café.
	you can watch the aeroplanes.
	(etc.)

or

There is	a café a restaurant a hotel	in near	Y,	which is quite cheap. which serves good food. in which you can have a rest.

59

6   Who will show you round?

A guide who knows a lot about	the ruins aeroplanes engines history (etc.)	will show you round.

or

No one shows you around.
You can go around on your own.

7   What can you see there?

The main things you can look at are . . . .

    EXAMPLE: The main things you can look at are the ruins of the Greek
                temples.

8   Do many visitors go to there?

Many/not many visitors go to Y.

9   How long is it worth spending at X?

It is worth spending	an hour a morning a whole day a week (etc.)	at X.

10   Why do people go there?

Many people Some people	go to Y for	relaxation. fun. a rest. (etc.)

Written Exercises

EXERCISE FOUR   Write out the following passage:

    (*a*) putting the verbs in brackets in the present simple tense;
    (*b*) completing the blanks where necessary with: *who, whom, which, that*
        Where the relative pronoun can be left out, write out the sentence
        without any change.

Edinburgh

Edinburgh Castle (be) a place . . . . (be) well worth visiting. It (stand) high above the city of Edinburgh and you (can get) a beautiful view of the city and the surrounding hills. Princes Street, ... (be) the main shopping centre, (lie) below the castle to the north. The visitors . . . . you (see) in Edinburgh Castle (come) from all over the world. One of the places . . . . tourists (find) most interesting (be) a special cemetery for dogs. The soldiers . . . . (live) in the castle (bury) their dogs in this cemetery. Below on Princes Street (be) another unusual thing . . . . attracts many visitors. It (be) a flower clock. The hands and the face of the clock (cover:*passive*) with flowers . . . . (change:*passive*) by the gardeners according to the season of the year.

Read through the following passage.

One of the most beautiful places I have visited is the ancient Greek city of Cyrene in Libya. Cyrene is about 300 kilometres east of Benghazi. There is an excellent modern road to Cyrene. When you get there, you can stay in a hotel, which is fairly cheap and comfortable. The ruins which are found there are very beautiful and interesting. Not many tourists go to Cyrene and you can spend a whole day quietly by yourself. The main things you can look at are the temples, the statues and the caves.

WORK ON
LE PARAGRAPH

1 Count the sentences in the Sample Paragraph which contain adjectival clauses and underline the adjectival clauses.

2 Leptis Magna is an ancient Roman city about 50 kilometres east of Tripoli. Most of what is written in the Sample Paragraph about Cyrene can be written about Leptis Magna except there is no hotel there and no caves. But there is a camp site.

Rewrite the sample paragraph so that it is about Leptis Magna making all the changes which are necessary.

:abulary Study

A Notice the preposition 'about' in the sentence:
Cyrene is *about* 300 kilometres east of Benghazi.

Here 'about' means 'approximately'. 'About' is used when there is no need or it is impossible to give an exact figure of distance, height, time or cost.

EXAMPLES: about ten miles away   about five o'clock
about 200 metres high   about £20

B   Study the following expressions of direction:

North
North East
East
South East
South
South West
West
North West

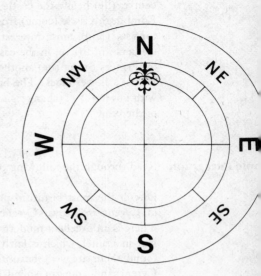

Student Writing   Now write a paragraph of your own describing a place you know which worth visiting.

Use the Preliminary Work, the Oral Practice, the Written Exercises a the Sample Paragraph to help you write your paragraph.

Try to write some sentences in your paragraph containing different types adjectival clause.

Correction

1   Read through your paragraph carefully checking the use of adjecti clauses and punctuation and prepositions.

2   Exchange your work with another student. You check his paragraph any mistakes and he will check your work.

Consolidation Work

GRAMMATICAL NOTE   Study this table giving the different types of adjectival clauses practis in Sections Nine and Ten.

		Refers to	Examples
Defining	Relative pronoun (subject)	People	The people who come here are usually interesting.
		Things	The shop that (which) sells newspapers is closed on Sundays.
	Relative pronoun (object)	People	The man (who, that) you met yesterday is my uncle.
		Things	The places (that, which) the tourists go to visit are quite near.
Non-defining	Relative pronoun (subject)	People	Ghandi, who led India to independence, is still remembered today.
		Things	Khartoum, which stands at the junction of the White Nile and the Blue Nile, is a modern city.
	Relative pronoun (object)	People	Our headmaster, whom you met yesterday, is going to retire at the end of this term.
		Things	Westminster Abbey, which most visitors to London go to see, was built hundreds of years ago.

EXERCISE FIVE   Rewrite the following sentences in the way shown in the example. Where necessary, put *who*, *whom* or *which* at the beginning of the adjectival clause.

> EXAMPLE: The place . . . . is about 100 kilometres west of London. (I am going to write about)
>
> The place *I am going to write about* is about 100 kilometres west of London.

1   The place . . . . is about 50 kilometres north-east of Leeds. (I am going to write about)
2   It is called York and it is a city . . . . (I have visited many times)
3   York still has its original walls for defence . . . . (were built about 600 years ago)
4   Some of the buildings . . . . are over 800 years old. (you can see in York)

63

5 The Children's Museum, ..., is the best-known museum in the city (contains an imitation street of York 100 years ago)
6 The University of York, ..., stands outside York in the country. (wa opened a few years ago)
7 The students, ..., come from all over Britain. (live in halls of residence
8 There are also foreign students . . . . (come from many different countrie in the world)

EXERCISE SIX Write complete sentences beginning with:

There is . . . ., or *there are* . . . .

EXAMPLE: An underground station near the museum.
            There is an underground station near the museum.

1 many places of historical interest in Iraq.
2 several markets in Baghdad.
3 many modern roads leading out of Baghdad.
4 a beautiful holiday camp near Arbil.
5 an interesting statue in the ancient city of Babylon.

GRAMMATICAL NOTE   Sentences beginning with 'there is . . . .' or 'there are . . . .' are often use when referring to something for the first time.

Subject: *Letter Writing*

Pretend that someone has written to you asking you to describe yourself. Write a letter in reply.

Note: There is no Oral Practice in this section.

Written Exercises

EXERCISE ONE   Read the following letter and answer the questions after it.

> 57, Hessle Mount
> Leeds 10
> 28th April, 1972
>
> Dear Ahmed,
>   Thank you for your letter of the 19th April, which I received a few days ago. In this letter you asked me to write a short description of myself. Here is a simple description which I have written for you.
>   I am eighteen years old, not very tall and I have long black hair. I wear very unusual clothes and my father often gets angry with me. He wants me to wear a jacket and tie. I am a student at Leeds University and I work hard before the exams. In my spare time I like sitting in the students' union and chatting with my friends. During term I share a flat with three friends. I have a lot of bright posters on the walls of my bedroom.
>   I hope to hear from you soon. Please write and tell me about yourself.
>   Yours sincerely
>   Peter

Questions

1 Who wrote this letter?
2 To whom is it written?
3 What is the address of the writer?
4 When was it written?
5 In his letter of the 19th April, what did Ahmed ask Peter to do?
6 How many paragraphs are there in this letter?
7 What does Peter write about in the first paragraph of his letter?
8 What does he ask Ahmed in the last paragraph?
9 Have you read the second paragraph of Peter's letter before? Where did you read it?

EXERCISE TWO In Section Four (see page 23) you were asked to write a description yourself. Use this description to write a letter similar to the letter in Exercise One. You can make the first and last paragraphs of your letter the same in Exercise One.

Sample Paragraph Read the following passage carefully. It is the Sample Paragraph in Section Four (page 22) rewritten with some sentences containing time clauses and adjectival clauses.

I am eighteen years old, not very tall and I have long black hair. I like wear unusual clothes, but, when my father sees me, he gets angry. He wants me to wear clothes which look more respectable. I am a student Leeds University, which is in the north of England. After I have attended my lectures in the morning, I like sitting in the students' union and chatting with my friends who have the same interests as me. I share a flat with three friends who were at school with me. The walls of my bedroom are covered with bright posters which make the room colourful.

WORK ON
SAMPLE PARAGRAPH
1 How many adjectival clauses are there in the Sample Paragraph? Underline each one or read them out.
2 How many time clauses are there in the Sample Paragraph? Underline each one or read them out.
3 Go back to your own corrected Paragraph Four and rewrite it in a similar way to this Sample Paragraph. Include some sentences containing adjectival clauses and some sentences containing time clauses. Write it out as a rough draft; that is not for handing to your teacher but for your own use.
4 Exchange the rough draft of your re-written Paragraph Four with another student. You check his work, he checks yours.

Student Writing Use the rough draft you have written as the second paragraph in a letter describing yourself. You can make the first and last paragraphs of your letter the same as in Exercise One (page 65), but put in your own name and address and the correct date.

Correction

1 Read your letter carefully and make sure the address, date and first and last paragraphs are correct. Check the second paragraph for any mistakes in copying from the rough draft.
2 Exchange your work with another student. He checks your letter and you check his.

solidation Work

1 Read your corrected letter to each other in pairs or in groups.
2 You have already written some other paragraphs. These can be used in a letter in a similar way to Paragraph Four.

EXAMPLES: Paragraph Two   Someone has written to you asking you to tell him what you do on your weekly holiday.
Paragraph Five   Someone has written to you asking you to tell him what you will do at the next public holiday.

3 Go back and re-read your own corrected Paragraphs Two and Five. Choose one of them and re-write it to include some sentences containing time clauses and some sentences containing adjectival clauses.
Exchange your re-written paragraph with another student. You check his work, he checks yours.

(*Question 4 is on page 68*).

67

4 In the following letter complete the blanks. Where a choice is given in a substitution table, choose the words that suit your letter.
Use your re-written paragraph (see 3 above) as the second paragraph in this letter.

Put in: address,
date.

Dear . . . .

Thank you for your letter of . . . ., which I

received   yesterday
            a few days ago.   In this letter you
            last week.

asked me to tell you about   my weekly holiday.
                          the next public holiday.

Some weeks ago
A few months ago   I wrote about this at school. Here is the
Not long ago

paragraph I wrote.
(*Put in here the paragraph you have re-written in* 3 *above.*)

I hope to hear from you soon. Please write and tell me

about your   weekly holiday.
            next public holiday.

Yours sincerely,

(*put your name here*)

Correction   When you have written your letter exchange it for a letter written by another student on a subject different to yours. You check his work, he checks yours.
Give it to your teacher to read.

68

¶12 Your Progress

SENTENCES   Here are three sentences from the Sample Paragraph in Section Two (on page 10):

> Every Sunday morning I get up at half-past nine. My wife makes the breakfast straight away. We have breakfast together.

Compare them with these sentences from the Sample Paragraph in Section Ten (on page 61):

> There is an excellent modern road to Cyrene. When you get there, you can stay in a hotel which is fairly cheap and comfortable.

You will notice that the sentences in Section Ten contain more complex structures than those in Section Two.

Compare your own corrected Paragraph Two with your own corrected Paragraph Ten. Is there a difference between the two? Are you using sentences with more complex structures?

SUBJECTS   Compare the subject matter of Paragraph Two:

> Write a paragraph about how you spent last night.

with the subject matter of Paragraph Nine:

> Write a paragraph about an occasion when you met someone who was boring, frightening or a nuisance.

You will notice that as this course goes on the subject matter is becoming more difficult, but you should be finding it easier to write about more difficult subjects.

MISTAKES   You will probably find that you are still making some mistakes in your writing. This should not worry you if you are making mistakes in *new* uses of language. You can often learn from these mistakes.

Are you still making the same mistakes you were making in Paragraphs One to Five? You must not make mistakes with tenses and pronouns. You can practise some of the exercises in Sections One to Five again.

Planning and Note Making   In this course, the Oral Practice and Written Exercises give you help in planning your paragraph. When you are writing a free paragraph (perhaps in an examination), you may find it helpful to make some notes before you write your paragraph.

69

EXERCISE ONE   Read through the Sample Paragraph A in Section Seven on page 37. Her
are some notes about this paragraph. Compare these notes with the Sampl
Paragraph sentence by sentence.

first time at school
five years old
did not want to go
taken by my grandfather
frightened in the playground
found another gate
ran home
my grandfather surprised to see me

EXERCISE TWO   Go back to the Sample Paragraph in Section Ten on page 61 and make
list of notes similar to those given above.

Here is a list of notes for the Sample Paragraph in Section Ten. Compa
it with what you have written.

Greek City of Cyrene in Libya
one of the most beautiful places I have visited
about 300 kms east of Benghazi
excellent, modern road to Cyrene
at Cyrene stay in a hotel
fairly cheap and comfortable
the ruins beautiful and interesting
very quiet—not many tourists
you can look at temples, statues and caves.

Sample Notes   Here are some notes followed by a Sample Paragraph on how a frier
and Paragraph   spends her day at work.
Read through the notes and Sample Paragraph carefully.

A friend called Mary
She is a Social Security Official
Social Security a government department
helps people who are very poor
she starts work at 8.30
makes a list of people to visit
visits the people on her list
makes notes during her visit
has lunch in a café
comes back to the office
writes reports on each person visited
finishes work at 5 p.m.

70

mple Paragraph (*based on above notes*)

I have a friend called Mary, who is a Social Security Official. Social Security is a government department which helps those people who are extremely poor. Mary starts work in her office at half-past eight in the morning. First she makes a list of people she must visit. Then she goes out and visits each person and makes notes during each visit. She has lunch in a café and returns to her office in the afternoon. She writes reports on each person or family she has visited. After she has finished her reports, usually about five o'clock, she leaves the office and gets the bus back home.

Student Writing

Write a paragraph on how a friend spends his or her day at work.
You may make a list of notes like the ones before the Sample Paragraph.
Try to use some of the structures you have been practising in Part Two of this course. Here is a list of them:

Time clauses with *when, while, after, before*:
  When she finishes work, she goes home.
  While she is visiting each family, she writes a report.
Adjectival clauses with relative pronoun subject (defining and non-defining):
  I have a friend called Mary, *who is a Social Security worker*.
  I know a man *who is very poor*.
Adjectival clauses with relative pronoun object (defining and non-defining):
  She writes a report on each family *she has visited*.
  London, *which is the largest city in England*, is a very interesting place to work in.

Correction

1 If you have made some notes check that you have included all the important points in your paragraph.
2 Check your paragraph carefully. Make sure that you have used time clauses and adjectival clauses correctly.
3 Exchange your work with another student. He checks your work and you check his.

71

Answers to Competition, page 47

Here are the other six changes. They can be given in any order but if ther are any mistakes in spelling or punctuation then no prize can be given.

After he had drawn a tree, he changed it to a flower.
After he had drawn a banana, he changed it to a cigarette.
After he had drawn a dog, he changed it to a cat.
After he had drawn a railway-station, he changed it to a police-station.
After he had drawn a clock at 9 o'clock, he changed it to a clock at 4 o'clock
After he had drawn a horse and cart, he changed it to a bus.

Part Three

Three more types of complex
sentence are introduced and there
is a variety of new structural work
and revision.

Increasing attention is given in the
subject matter to logical sequence
and to expressing opinions.

There is no consolidation work
after sections.

Subject: *A Dream*
Preliminary work about noun clauses (statements).

EXERCISE ONE   Read the following sentences:
1   I had turned into a toothbrush.
2   My uncle was sitting on a crocodile.
3   I had become invisible.
4   The walls of my room were moving.
5   My friend had a horse's head.
6   I could walk on the ceiling.
7   The people in the picture came alive.
8   The boy's feet were like a donkey's.

Answer these questions:
(*a*) Do you think the above sentences are unusual?
(*b*) Why are they strange?
(*c*) How could you use them in speech or in writing?

Answers to the questions:
(*a*) Yes, they are unusual.
(*b*) They are strange because they speak of things which are either impossil
or highly unlikely.
(*c*) It is very easy to use them in speech or in writing by putting some wor
in front of them:
    I dreamed that . . . .
    I thought that . . . .
    I pretended that . . . .
    I imagined that . . . .

EXAMPLE: 1. I dreamed that I had turned into a toothbrush.

Write out the sentences 1–8 putting any of the phrases given above
front of them. Follow the example.

GRAMMATICAL NOTE   The second part of each of the sentences you have written is called a *no*
clause (statement). The word 'that' is often left out. For example:
    I dreamed I was able to fly.

EXERCISE TWO   Rewrite the following sentences putting the words in brackets before ea
sentence. Change the tense of the verbs in the first sentence into the p:
in the way shown in the examples.

74

Rules for tense changes:
Present simple becomes past simple.
Past simple becomes past perfect.
Present continuous becomes past continuous.

EXAMPLES: I *see* a strange shape. (I thought . . . .)
I thought I *saw* a strange shape.

I *heard* a noise. (I imagined that . . . .)
I imagined that I *had heard* a noise.

I *am walking* in a dark cave. (I dreamed . . . .)
I dreamed that I *was walking* in a dark cave.

1 I am in a strange house. (I dreamed that . . . .)
2 I do not know the house. (I thought . . . .)
3 An old friend comes in. (I dreamed . . . .)
4 He is looking for me. (He said that . . . .)
5 He wants to tell me something terrible. (He said . . . .)
6 He discovered a terrible secret. (I knew that . . . .)
7 I feel very afraid. (I dreamed that . . . .)
8 He is about to tell me the secret. (I imagined that . . . .)
9 I hear my mother calling. (I thought . . . .)
10 My breakfast is nearly ready. (She was saying that . . . .)

¶13

Subject: *A Dream*

Tell the story of a dream you have had. Or if you cannot remember one, tell the story of a dream which someone else has told you.

LANGUAGE
TEACHING POINTS

Noun clauses (statements) with 'that' or no introducer
Past simple tense
Connectives: *Later, At this point, Just then*
Revision of adverbs of frequency
Revision of pronoun reference

Oral Practice

Ask each other and answer the following questions:

1 How often do you dream?

I dream	every night.
	occasionally.
	not very often.
	after I have eaten a big meal.

I do not dream very often.

76

2 Do you remember your dreams?

        rarely
        occasionally
I   sometimes   remember my dreams.
        always
        never

3 When did you last have a dream?

                last night.
                a few nights ago.
I had a dream   one night last week.
                one night last month.
                (etc.)

4 What did you dream about?

              I was in a strange house.
              my friend was fighting with me.
I dreamed that   I had found £1,000.
              a strange animal was chasing me.
              (etc.)

(*try to say something about a dream you have had*)

5 What happened then?

6 When did you wake up?

7 *Think of an actual dream you have had.*
Where were you?
What happened?
When did you wake up?

Possible ways to begin your answers:
   I'm not sure, but I think that . . . .
   I felt that I . . . .
   I thought that I . . . .
   Just as . . . ., I woke up.

8 Do you tell your dreams to your friends?

        sometimes
Yes, I occasionally tell my dreams to my friends.
        usually

No, I never speak about my dreams.

Written Exercises

EXERCISE THREE Rewrite the following passage putting all the verbs in brackets into the past simple tense.

A few nights ago I (dream) that a stranger (come) to my house and (take) some gramophone records without permission. In my dream I (hurry) after him and (follow) him to his house. I (dream) that I (knock) at the door of his house. When I (knock) at the door, someone who (have) his face covered with a black cloth (open) it. I (ask) him for my records. The man at the door (say) he (know) nothing about them. He (hand) me some books and (say) I (have to) read them before the morning. At that moment I (wake) up. Some books (be) on the floor beside my bed. I (know) that they (be) not mine.

EXERCISE FOUR Rewrite the following passage leaving out the words 'I dreamed that' ' thought that' 'I imagined that' wherever possible.

Last night I dreamed that I was climbing a steep mountain. I thought that round my waist there was a rope which was tied to the guide in front of me. Then I dreamed that it grew darker and the rope in front of me became loose. I imagined that I pulled the rope towards me and soon found the other end. I imagined that I was alone on the mountain. Just then I woke up.

You will have found that it is possible to leave out the words 'I dreamed that' 'I thought that' 'I imagined that' every time it occurs except the first.

Note: In writing about a dream you need to use the words 'I dreamed that' only once at the beginning but you can repeat the words such as 'I dreamed' 'I thought' or 'I imagined', when you want to remind the reader that you are re-telling a dream.

Vocabulary Study   Below is a list of words connected with sleeping and dreaming:

go to sleep	a sleepless night
fall asleep	to toss and turn in one's sleep
sleep deeply	have a nap
sleep lightly	have a siesta
a daydream	have forty winks
a nightmare	walk in one's sleep

Sample Paragraph   Read through the following passage.

A few weeks ago I dreamed a very unusual dream. I dreamed that I was walking along a street and all the friends I had ever known were walking behind me. I was leading them and telling jokes and singing. I thought that the other people in the street would be angry, but they started to laugh and to clap. Later we all went into a big hotel and I stood up and made a speech. At this point all my friends became angry and started to chase me. I ran up and up flights of stairs and at the top came to a door which was locked. I felt very afraid and thought they would catch me. Just then I woke up.

1 Rewrite this paragraph beginning:
'A few weeks ago William dreamed a very unusual dream.'
Use any name you choose of a boy *or* a girl.
Make all the necessary changes to 'I' 'me' 'my' and 'we'.
2 Count the number of noun clauses in the Sample Paragraph.
3 Note the use of the words *later, at this point, Just then*. These phrases are commonly used in narratives to emphasise the order in which things happened.

tudent Writing Write a paragraph about a dream you have had.
You may make notes as suggested in Section Twelve (page 70) to help you. Use the Preliminary Work, the Oral Practice and the Written Exercises to help you write your own paragraph.
Make sure you use some noun clauses (statements) in your paragraph.

Correction

1 Read through your paragraph carefully. Check the tenses and the forms of the verbs you have used. If you made rough notes make sure you included all the important points in the notes.
2 Exchange your paragraph with another student. You check his paragraph for any mistakes and the other student checks your work.

79

Subject: *Doing something wrong when you were young*
Preliminary work about noun clauses (questions)

EXERCISE ONE   Study the changes made in the following sentences when they are joined
to the words 'My father asked me . . . .'

My father asked me:
1   Why are you out so late?
2   Where have you been?
3   Who were you with?
4   What have you been doing?
5   Have you been smoking?
6   Why do you go out so often?

1   My father asked me why I was out so late.
2   My father asked me where I had been.
3   My father asked me who I had been with.
4   My father asked me what I had been doing.
5   My father asked me if I had been smoking.
6   My father asked my why I went out so often.

GRAMMATICAL NOTE   The second part of each of these sentences—the original question—
called a *noun clause (question)*.
There are five changes made when these sentences follow the words 'My
father asked me . . . .'.

1   There is no question mark.
2   The order of the words is changed from a question to a statement. If 'do'
is used as an auxiliary verb to make a question, it is left out.
EXAMPLE: Why *do you look* sick?
My father asked me why *I looked* sick.
3   The tense of the verbs is changed:
Present simple becomes past simple.
Present perfect becomes past perfect.
Past simple becomes past perfect.
Present perfect continuous becomes past perfect continuous.
4   The pronoun 'you' in the question becomes 'I' after 'My father asked
me . . . .'
5   When a question does not begin with a question word like 'why' 'what'
'who' (etc.) then you must put in the word 'if'.
EXAMPLES: Have you been smoking?
My father asked me *if* I had been smoking.
Are you telling the truth?
My father asked me *if* I was telling the truth.

EXERCISE TWO Rewrite the following questions in the way shown in the example.

Who has spilled coffee on the chair? (My mother wanted to know . . . .)
My mother wanted to know *who had spilled coffee on the chair*.

Make all the necessary changes to verb forms, word order, tenses and pronouns. If in doubt, look back at the examples in Exercise One. Note that 'will' becomes 'would'.

1   Who has spilled coffee on the chair? (My mother asked me . . . .)
2   Where were you at tea-time? (My father wanted to know . . . .)
3   Who did you have in the house with you? (My mother asked me . . . .)
4   Did you spill the coffee? (My father asked me . . . .)
5   Did your friend spill the coffee? (My mother wanted to know . . . .)
6   Are you telling the truth? (My father asked me . . . .)
7   Why did you not clean it up? (My mother asked me . . . .)
8   Are you going to clean it up? (My father asked me. . . . .)

¶14

Subject: *Doing Something Wrong*

Write a paragraph telling the story of how you did something wrong when you were young. For example, telling a lie, breaking something in the house, going somewhere you were told not to go, or taking something you had been told not to take or anything you choose. Say whether you were found out or not.

LANGUAGE   Noun clauses (questions)
LEARNING POINTS   Tenses in noun clauses (questions)
Pronoun agreement in noun clauses (questions)
Word order in noun clauses (questions)
Past perfect continuous tense

Oral Practice   Ask and answer the following questions:

1   Have you ever done something wrong?

            often
Yes, I have   frequently   done something wrong.
            occasionally

No, I have never done anything wrong.

82

2   Have you ever told a lie?

Yes, I have $\begin{array}{l}\text{sometimes}\\\text{occasionally}\end{array}$ told a lie.

No, I have never told a lie.

3   Can you remember something wrong which you did?
Once, when I . . . ., I . . . .

EXAMPLE: Once, when I lived in the country, I climbed into someone's garden.

4   Did you do this alone?
Yes, I did.
No, I did it with . . . .

EXAMPLE: No, I did it with some friends.

5

When you were young, did you ever
- smoke a cigarette?
- break a cup or a plate?
- spill something?
- break a clock?
- lose money?
- take something?
- go somewhere without permission?
  (etc.)

Yes, I remember once that I . . . .

EXAMPLE: Yes, I remember once that I took my brother's shirt and wore it to a party.

6

Did anyone ask you if you had
- smoked a cigarette?
- broken a cup?
- lost the shopping money?
- spent the money on sweets?
  (etc.)

Yes, my $\begin{array}{l}\text{mother}\\\text{father}\\\text{brother}\\\text{(etc.)}\end{array}$ asked me if I had . . . .

7

Did anyone ask you
- where you had been?
- where you had got the X?
  (etc.)

8

Did you tell $\begin{array}{l}\text{your mother/father}\\\text{your sister/brother}\\\text{a friend}\\\text{(etc.)}\end{array}$ what you had done?

Yes, I told my brother what I had done.
No, I did not tell anyone what I had done.

83

9   Were you ashamed of what you had done?

Yes, I was ashamed
of what I had done.
No, I was not ashamed

10 Did you do something wrong which was never discovered?

Yes, once I . . . . and I was never discovered.

EXAMPLE: Yes, once I burnt a hole in the garden fence and I was never
discovered.

Written Exercises

EXERCISE THREE   Rewrite the following passage putting the verbs in brackets in the correct
tense.

I remember once when I (be) in primary school, I (have) a friend who
(have) an older brother. This brother (be) in India and (bring) back with
him some Indian cigars. My friend (take) some of the cigars and we (smoke)
them in an empty house. When I (get) home that evening, I (feel) very
sick. My father (notice) this and (ask) me what I (do). He (ask) me if I
(smoke). When I (say) that I (not smoke), he (reply) that I (tell) lies. My
friend's mother (come) to our house at that moment and (tell) my father
what we (do). My friend (confess) everything and I (be punished) severely
both for smoking and for telling lies.

Sample Paragraphs

Read through the following passages.

A   When I was at primary school, I was given a shilling every day for my
lunch. Sometimes I cheated and instead of buying lunch at school, I
bought sweets in a nearby shop. One day my mother came to the school
to see my teacher. The teacher asked my mother why I did not buy lunch
every day. When my mother heard this, she realised immediately what I
had been doing. She asked me what I had done with the money. When I
told her that I had been buying sweets, she became very angry and warned
me not to do it again.

B   When I was young, I had a very bad temper. I did something once which I
am now very ashamed of. My older sister's fiancé was in the army and every
week my sister bought cigarettes for her fiancé which she kept in a drawer
in her bedroom. One day I had a quarrel with my sister. My mother and
father were out and my sister was looking after me. I wanted to stay up and
watch television, but my sister insisted that it was time to go to bed. I
became very angry and went to her bedroom with a pair of scissors. I cut
all the cigarettes into small pieces. My sister discovered what I had done and
burst out crying. When my father came home, my sister told him what I
had done. My father asked me if my sister was telling the truth. I could not

84

deny that I had cut up the cigarettes. I was severely punished and I did not get any more pocket money until I had paid for the cigarettes.

SAMPLE PARAGRAPHS

1 Find the sentences in the Sample Paragraphs containing noun clauses (statements) and underline the noun clauses. There is one noun clause (statement) in Sample Paragraph A and two noun clauses (statements) in Sample Paragraph B.

2 Find the sentences in the Sample Paragraph A containing noun clauses (questions) and underline the noun clauses. There are three noun clauses (questions) in Sample Paragraph A and three in Sample Paragraph B.

Vocabulary Study

A Notice the difference between the following expressions:
   to be naughty, to do something naughty
   Used when speaking to young children who have done something wrong but not really serious.
   to do something wrong
   When used about young people, it usually means something not very serious. When used about older people, it can refer to more serious things.
   to commit a crime
   to do something which is against the laws of a country.
   to commit a sin, to sin
   to do something which is against the laws of a religion.

B Note the constructions used after the following verbs:

   accuse: The policeman accused *me of breaking* the windows.
   confess: I confessed *that I had taken it.* (noun clause statement)
   　　　　　　　　　what I had done. (noun clause question)
   admit: He admitted *that he had done wrong.*
   　　　　　　　what he had done.
   deny: He denied *that he had done wrong.*
   　　　　　　what he had said.
   feel ashamed: I felt ashamed *of what I had done.*

Student Writing

Now write a paragraph of your own about something you did which was wrong. Use the Preliminary Work, the Oral Practice and the Written Exercises and the Sample Paragraphs to help you write your paragraph. Try to include some noun clauses (questions) in your paragraph.

85

Correction

1 Read through your paragraph. Check the word order and the use of tense in any noun clauses (questions) you have used.

2 Exchange your work with another student. You check his paragraph for any mistakes and the other student checks your work.

¶15 Subject: *Your Future*
Preliminary work about 'if'-clauses and adverbials of time.

EXERCISE ONE Join the following groups of words together to make a sentence in the way shown in the example.

EXAMPLES: I have enough money.   I travel in many different countries.
If I have enough money, I will travel in many different countries.

Note that in this kind of sentence you can use either 'I will' or 'I shall'.

My future
1 I pass in mathematics.   I become a doctor.
2 I become a doctor.   I work in a hospital.
3 I make enough money.   I have my own clinic in the evenings.
4 I save more money.   I go abroad to take another degree.
5 I have a good job.   I get married in ten years' time.
6 I have a son.   I want him to become a doctor.

GRAMMATICAL NOTE The part of this sentence in italics is called an *'if'-clause*.
If I pass my exams, I will go to university.

When you are speaking about things in the future which you think are likely to happen, you use the simple present tense in the 'if'-clause, usually followed by future tense in the main clause.

When the 'if'-clause comes first in the sentence, it is separated from the main clause by a comma.
If I pass my exams, I will go to university.

When the 'if'-clause comes after the main clause, there is no comma.
I will go to university if I pass my exams.

POSITION OF ADVERBIALS OF TIME Adverbials of time and frequency can come at the beginning or at the end of a sentence.

This time next year I will be on holiday.
I will be on holiday *this time next year*.

Usually I go to Scotland for my holidays.
I go to Scotland for my holidays *usually*.

Adverbials of frequency like 'sometimes' 'often' 'usually' can also come before the verb.
I *usually* go to Scotland for my holidays.

'Never' and 'ever' always come in this position.

Have you *ever* been to Italy?

I have *never* been to Italy.

EXERCISE TWO Rewrite the following sentences putting the adverbials given in bracket
in all the different possible positions.

1   Tom will be on holiday.   (in eight months' time)
2   He is hoping to go to Spain.   (next year)
3   He goes to Scotland.   (usually)
4   He will be sitting on the beach.   (in the first fortnight of August)
5   He sits on the beach in sunny weather.   (always)
6   It is autumn.   (now)
7   Tom is dreaming about next year.   (already)
8   He has been to Spain before.   (never)

¶15 **Subject**: *Your Future*
Write a paragraph about what you think you will be doing in the future. For example, five or six years from now.

LANGUAGE
ARNING POINTS

'If'-clauses containing present simple tense
Future continuous tense
Noun clauses (statements)
Adjectival clauses
Order of adverbials of time
Definite and indefinite articles

Oral Practice   Ask and answer each of the following questions.

1   How old are you now?
I am . . . . years old.

2   Are you working or studying?

3   What do you think you will be doing in . . . . years' time?

In . . . . years' time I think I	will be studying at/in . . . .
	will be working as . . . .
	will have my first job . . . .
	will be married.
	will be living in . . . .
	will be visiting . . . .

4   Is there something special you want to do in the future?

In . . . . years' time		go to England/the States/India (etc.).
Next year		pass my . . . . (name of an exam).
In the summer		get a good job as . . . .
In the future	I want to	train as a dentist/teacher (etc.).
		go to university.
		get a job in the holiday as . . . .
		become a really good football player.

5   Is there something you must do if you want to do this?

Yes, if I want to . . . . ,		save up enough money.
		pass my exams.
		go to university.
(say your answer to question 4),	I will have to	do well at maths.
		go to night-school.
		work in the holidays.
		spend a lot of time in training.
		(etc.)

EXAMPLES: Yes, if I want to go to the States in five years' time, I will have
to pass my examinations.

Yes, if I want to become a really good football player, I will
have to spend a lot of time in training.

6

> If you become an engineer/a doctor/a civil servant,
> If you succeed in going to England/the States/India, | what will you do then?
> If you succeed in getting a good job,
>   (etc.)

If I become . . . ., If I succeed in . . . .,	I will	work in a government school. work hard to get promotion. save up to get my own business. visit as many places as possible. study at university. live in London/Calcutta/New York. get married in a few years' time. (etc.)

7 When will you get married?

If I	pass all my exams, get a good degree, meet the right man/woman, get a good job, get promotion, save up enough money, fall in love,	I will get married	at about the age of twenty-five. (etc.) in about . . . . years' time.

8 What will you do if you cannot do what you want to do?

If I cannot . . . ., (*say what you want to do*)	I will	leave school and go to work. go back to my village. feel angry for the rest of my life. work with my father. help my children to . . . . encourage my brother/sister to . . . .

EXAMPLES: If I cannot get a good job as a civil servant, I will go back to my village.

If I cannot become a really good football-player, I will encourage my brother to train as a football-player.

Written Exercises

EXERCISE THREE   Write out the following passage with correct punctuation.

i am sixteen years old now and i am studying at a secondary technical schoc
if I pass my exams next june I shall go to a polytechnic in september ane
study there for another four years if i finish my studies at the polytechni
successfully i shall become an engineer i am interested in bridge buildin
and i hope to get a job with a large bridge building company

EXERCISE FOUR   Rewrite the following passage filling in the blanks with: 'a' 'an' or 'the
Do not write anything where 'a' 'an' or 'the' are wrong.
EXAMPLE: I shall go to . . . . Khartoum University.
           I shall go to Khartoum University.

I want to become . . . . teacher. If I pass my examinations next year,
shall go to . . . . Bradford University. At . . . . University of Bradford,
shall take . . . . degree in . . . . French and . . . . German. When I get m
degree, I shall go to . . . . teachers' training college, but I do not knov
yet which one. After I have finished at . . . . teachers' training college,
shall become . . . . teacher.

Sample Paragraphs

Read through the following passages.

A   The following passage was written by a young man in England.

I am seventeen years old now and I left school two years ago. I work as ar
apprentice in a garage. If I complete my apprenticeship successfully,
will become a motor mechanic in three years' time. I will still be workin{
in the garage I am working in now. If I can save up enough money, I wil
buy a car of my own. I have a girl friend and we hope to get married when I
finish my apprenticeship. If we get married, we will have to live at firs
with my girl friend's parents. Later, if we can save up enough money, we
will buy our own furniture and get a house of our own.

B   The following passage was written by a girl in England.

I am sixteen years old and I am studying at Leeds Girls High School
I have never been out of England and I really want to visit France. If I
do well in my exams at the end of this year, my parents have promised
to help me. If they give me enough money, I will spend all next summe
in France. I will ask my French teacher to write to a family in France. If
she finds a French family who are willing to take me, I will go and stay with
them. If they have a daughter who wants to visit England, she can come and
stay with me the year after. If I succeed in my plan, I will be staying in
France next summer. If I do not succeed, I will try again the following year

WORK ON
SAMPLE PARAGRAPHS

1   Count the number of 'if'-clauses in Sample Paragraph A.
2   Count the number of 'if'-clauses in Sample Paragraph B.

If you are going to write about the job you may do in the future, you will need some of these words.

career: the way you will make your living. Do you know what the job you hope to do in the future is called in English?

apprenticeship: the time you have to spend learning a trade, e.g. becoming a baker, a bricklayer, a mechanical engineer.

profession: this is used to describe jobs like teacher, lawyer, doctor.

qualified: this is sometimes used before a trade or profession to show that the person has completed his training, e.g. a qualified accountant.

Student Writing Now write a paragraph of your own about what you think you will be doing in the future. Use the Oral Practice, Written Exercises and the Sample Paragraphs to help you write your paragraph. Try to include some 'if'-clauses in your paragraph.

Correction

1 Read through your paragraph carefully and check the correct form of verbs, the use of the future continuous tense and punctuation in sentences containing 'if'-clauses.

2 Exchange your work with another student. You check his paragraph for any mistakes and the other student checks your work.

¶16

Subject: *A Difficult Decision in the Past*

Write a paragraph about a difficult decision you made in the past and which you still remember clearly. Describe how you made your decision and say what were the results. If you cannot remember a decision of your own, write about someone else.

LANGUAGE
LEARNING POINTS

'Because' clauses

Catenatives: I *wanted to learn to dance.*

Instead of + present participle

Derek bought a motorcycle *instead of buying* a car.

Oral Practice

Ask each other and answer the following questions.

First decide whether you will write about yourself or another person.

1   How old are you now?

How old is X now?

(If you are writing about someone else, use 'he' or 'she' in all the questions and answers.)

94

2   What are you going to write about?

                                                              sell . . . .

                                                              buy . . . .

I am going to write about how I decided to   learn to . . . .

                                                              study . . . .

                                                              visit . . . .

    EXAMPLES: I am going to write about how I decided to learn to dance.

                  I am going to write about how my friend decided to buy a bicycle.

3   When did this happen?

                                                              living in . . . .

It happened . . . . years ago when I was   studying in . . . .

                                                            working at/as . . . .

    EXAMPLE: It happened two years ago when I was studying at secondary
                school.

4   What did you/X want to do?

                        learn to dance.

                        buy a motorcycle.

I wanted to   visit France.

                        do a job in the holidays.

                        change my subject.

                            (*or whatever you are writing about*)

    And why?

                        wanted to go to dances.

                        was interested in motorcycles.

                        had never been abroad before.

Because I   needed more money.

                        liked English better than history.

                        (etc.)

5   Why was it difficult to make the decision?

was worried about	learning to dance
	buying a motorcycle
	visiting France
	doing a job in the holidays
	changing my subject
	(*or whatever you are writing about*)

because I	felt shy.
	thought motorcycles were dangerous.
	was not very good at French.
	would not be able to go away.
	might find English difficult.
	(etc.)

6 Why did you need to make a decision?
                  a friend was going to go to dancing lessons.
                  there was a cheap motorcycle for sale.
     Because   it might be my last chance.
                  there were holiday jobs at local factories.
                  the university had written to me.
                  (etc.)

7 How did you decide in the end?
   I discussed it with my friends/parents (etc.).
   I thought about it for several days before I made up my mind.

8
                                you
   Do you feel now that   he   did the right thing?
                                she
   Yes, I do.
   No, I do not.

Written Exercises

EXERCISE ONE   Join the following pairs of sentences with 'because' as in the example.

EXAMPLE: Harry wanted to become a guitarist in a pop-group.
         He thought he would make a lot of money.

         Harry wanted to become a guitarist in a pop-group *because h*
         thought he would make a lot of money.

1 At the age of sixteen Harry wanted to join a pop-group.
   He was an excellent guitarist.
2 He thought the life of a pop-star was exciting.
   He had seen them on television.
3 His father wanted him to become an apprentice electrician.
   This job was more secure.
4 His mother wanted him to stay at home.
   She was afraid of the future.
5 His girl friend wanted him to join a pop-group.
   She knew he was a really good guitarist.
6 Harry decided to leave home and join a pop-group.
   He thought he would be successful and make a lot of money.

EXERCISE TWO   Join the following pairs of sentences with 'instead of' and make all the
               necessary changes as shown in the example.

EXAMPLE: Derek decided to buy a motorcycle.
         He decided not to buy a car.

         Derek decided to buy a motorcycle *instead of buying a car.*

1 Derek's friends advised him to put his money in the bank.
   They advised him not to buy a motorcycle.

2 His father asked him to buy a car.
  He asked Derek not to buy a motorcycle.
3 Derek's girl friend told him to buy a record-player.
  She told him not to buy a motorcycle.
4 Derek's mother advised him to make up his own mind.
  She advised him not to listen to anyone else.
5 In the end Derek decided to buy the record-player.
  He decided not to buy the motorcycle.
6 His girl friend was pleased that he had taken her advice.
  He had not listened to other people.

ple Paragraphs   Read through the following passages.

A   I am now eighteen years old. I am going to write about how I learned to
     dance. It happened three years ago when I was fifteen. I was living in London
     and studying in secondary school. I wanted to learn to dance because I
     wanted to go to dances. On the other hand I did not want to go to the classes
     because I felt shy. I needed to make a decision because a friend of mine was
     just starting to go to dancing lessons. His mother had arranged for me to go
     with him. I discussed it with my friend. We decided it would be better
     going together instead of going on our own. When we arrived, my friend
     did not want to go in. But I quickly rang the door bell and the decision was
     made. I feel that I did the right thing because now I always enjoy going to
     dances and parties.

B   I am now twenty-two years old. I am going to write about how I decided
     to study English at university. It happened five years ago when I was living
     in Bristol and in my last year at secondary school. I had got a place at the
     University of Cambridge. I could study either history or English. I needed
     to make up my mind quickly because the University had written to me
     asking for a decision. I wanted to study history because I was good at it
     and I thought I would get a better degree. On the other hand I was really
     more interested in English. In the end I decided to study English instead of
     studying history. I feel now that I did the right thing because I enjoyed
     studying English and I got a good degree.

WORK ON
LE PARAGRAPHS
     1   Count the number of 'because'-clauses in Paragraph A.
     2   Count the number of 'because'-clauses in Paragraph B.

97

Vocabulary Study

A   Study the following expressions containing the word 'mind'.

      to make up one's mind : to decide on something

      to change one's mind : to change a decision or opinion

      to keep in mind : }

      to bear in mind : }   to remember

      to have in mind : to intend to do something

      it's in your mind : you are imagining it

      Mind out ! : Take care!

B   For words relating to jobs and careers look again at the Vocabulary Stud
for Section Fifteen on page 93.

Student Writing   Now write a paragraph of your own about a decision in the past. Use th
Oral Practice, Written Exercises and the Sample Paragraphs to help yo
write your paragraph. Try and include some 'because'-clauses in you
paragraph.

Correction

1   Read through your paragraph carefully and check spelling, punctuatior
the correct use of 'because'-clauses and the use of 'instead of'.

2   Exchange your work with another student. You check his paragraph for an
mistakes and the other student checks your work.

¶17

Subject: *Being Cheated*

Write a paragraph about an occasion when you or someone you know was cheated.

Tenses: past simple, past continuous
          can/could, will/would in noun clauses
Revision of clauses practised in earlier Sections.
Three part sentences.
Punctuation.

Oral Practice   Ask and answer the following questions:

1   Have you ever been cheated?

                                          a few weeks ago.
                                          last year.
Yes, I remember I was cheated   last summer.
                                              (etc.)

No, I do not remember being cheated.
But a friend of mine was cheated last year (etc.).

99

2 Where were you?
was X?

(*If you write about someone else, use 'he' or 'she' in all your questions and answers.*)

X		on holiday in . . . .
I	was	shopping in . . . .
		at a big fair.
		on a train/bus.
		(etc.)

3 And what were you doing?

I was		buying a ticket for . . . .
We were		buying some . . . .
		walking in the street . . . .
	just	travelling to . . . .
		sitting in a café . . . .
		selling . . . .
		waiting for . . . .

4 What happened then?

						playing cards.
			man			playing . . . .
I	noticed	a	woman	who	was	offering to buy . . . .
We	overheard	some	men		were	offering to sell . . . .
			women			standing with a camera.
						(etc.)

5 Who did you meet?

			asked us to . . . .
			offered to sell . . . .
I	met	a man	who	wanted to take my photograph.
We		a woman		invited us to play cards.
				offered to change some money.
				offered to sell us some black market goods.

EXAMPLE: We met a man who offered to sell us some cheap cigarettes.

6   What did the man/woman tell you?

The	man woman	said that	he she	would	take our photographs. show us a trick. buy . . . . from us. sell me . . . . take him to . . . . show us . . . . get us . . . . (etc.)

EXAMPLE: The woman said that she would get us some cheap cigarettes.

7   Why did you believe him?

I believed him because I was stupid.

I believed him because I	thought hoped	he/she was honest. we would make money. we would get . . . . cheaply.

8   How were you cheated?

I was cheated because

he gave us money which was useless.
he gave us very little money.
the photographs were blank pieces of paper.
the cards were marked on the back.
she took us to the wrong place.
he went into the house and out through the back
door.
(etc.)

9   What did you do about it?
(*Choose one answer.*)
I walked away and felt very stupid.
I went to the police.
We laughed at our own stupidity.
I went back to look for the woman.
I ran after the man.
    (etc.)

Written Exercises

EXERCISE ONE   Punctuate the following passage correctly.

last summer i visited london for the first time usually i went out with my
friends but one day they were all busy and i went out on my own i walked
round the centre of london and finished at buckingham palace i wanted to
get to victoria station i did not know how far it was and i took a taxi the

journey from buckingham palace to victoria station took half-an-hour whe
i got back and told my friends about my taxi ride they were amazed becaus
it is only ten minutes walk from buckingham palace to victoria station i ha
been cheated by the taxi driver who had realised that i was a tourist an
had taken me all over the place

EXERCISE TWO Rewrite the following paragraph putting the verbs in brackets in th
correct tense. Use the passive voice where necessary.

Last summer, when Tom and Peter (be) on holiday in Edinburgh, the
(walk) in the gardens beside Princes Street. A man (come) up to them an
(ask) for a light for his cigarette. He (begin) talking to them and (say) h
(know) a place where they (can get) cigarettes very cheaply. They (become
interested because they (think) they were going to get a bargain. The ma
(ask) them to follow him, (take) them to an old house behind the garden
and (ask) them to give him £1. He (say) he (will bring) the cigarettes in fiv
minutes. They (wait) for half-an-hour and the man (not come) back
They (go) into the house and (find) it (be) empty. The man (walk) throug
the house and out the back door. They (realise) that they (cheat).

Sample Paragraphs Read through the following passages.

A Many years ago, when I was a young boy, I went on holiday with a frien
to Liverpool. We spent one day walking through the centre of the cit
looking at the buildings. In Lime Street, which is a famous street in Liver
pool, we were stopped by a man who offered to take our photograph. H
said it would be ready in a few minutes and that we would not need to wait
We believed him because he looked honest. He put the photographs in a
envelope and said we must leave them for half-an-hour because the photo
graphs would be spoiled if we took them out before then. We paid him
fifteen pence, took the envelope and went on our way. Half-an-hour late
we stopped at a café and opened the envelope. It contained two pieces o
blank paper. We had been cheated. We laughed at our foolishness and
threw the pieces of paper away.

B I remember I was cheated three years ago. I was shopping in London
and as I was walking along a street I noticed some men who were playing
cards. I went over because I felt curious. One man was throwing three
cards upside down onto a table. Only one of the cards was an ace. If you
found the ace, you won a lot of money. The men who were playing seemed to
find the ace every time. The man, who was standing next to me, said I could
easily win a lot of money. I believed him because I was stupid. I leaned over
put £2 on a card and lost it immediately. I was cheated because all the men
were working together. They only pretended to win because they wanted
people to bet. I felt very foolish because I had been so easily tricked.

Study the following sentences.

Sample Paragraph A:

We paid him fifteen pence, took the envelope and went on our way.

Sample Paragraph B:

I leaned over, put £2 on a card and lost it immediately.

You will notice these sentences are made up of three simple sentences. The first part of the sentence ends with a comma and the third part begins with 'and'. This kind of three part sentence is common in English. Can you find another example of this kind of sentence in Exercise Two on page 102.

Write out the following groups of three sentences in one sentence as in the examples above.

1 The man asked us to wait.
   He went into the house.
   He closed the door.

2 We waited at the door.
   We chatted to one another.
   We began to be impatient.

3 We decided that something was wrong.
   We went up to the house.
   We knocked at the door.

4 We tried the handle.
   The door opened.
   We went in.

5 We shouted loudly.
   We looked in every room.
   We finally realised the house was empty.

6 We realised we had been cheated.
   We laughed at our foolishness.
   We resolved never to be cheated so easily again.

ocabulary Work   Make sure you know the meaning of the words in italics.

A *cheat* is someone who deceives you.

A person is often cheated because he is looking for a *bargain*—that is he hopes to buy something very cheaply.

People are often cheated in a *black market*—a place where goods are sold against the law.

If you *bet* (e.g. play cards for money), you may be cheated.

A *confidence trickster* is a man who makes money by cheating people. The men in Sample Paragraphs A and B are confidence tricksters.

103

Student Writing Now write a paragraph of your own about being cheated.

Use the Oral Practice, the Written Exercises and the Sample Paragrap
to help you write your paragraph.

Try to include some of the clauses you have been practising in Part Thr
in your paragraph.

noun clauses (statement and question)

'if'-clauses

'because'-clauses.

Correction

1 Read through your paragraph carefully and check spelling, punctuatio
and correct use of tenses.

2 Exchange your work with another student. You check his paragraph fo
any mistakes and the other student checks your work.

¶18 Revision

Review

1 Choose any *one* subject from the first five Sections in Part One of this course and write another paragraph on the same subject.

2 Try to include in your new paragraph some sentences containing:
adjectival clauses
noun clauses (statement and question)
'if'-clauses
'because'-clauses

3 When your teacher gives you back this paragraph, compare it with your first paragraph on the same subject and see how much your written English has improved.

Free Paragraph

1 Write a paragraph on *one* of the following subjects:

The thing you most like doing, e.g. going on holiday, making dresses, shopping, playing football, etc. Try to say why you like it and what benefits you get from it.

Your family. Write about your father, mother, brothers and sisters. Say how they all get on with one another and write about anything that causes trouble.

Your school and your friends.

The thing you most look forward to doing in your future life. Say what it is and why you look forward to it.

A happy memory in the past. Say what it was and why you remember it particularly.